The Golf Masters Series

Gary Player
with Mike Wade

BUNKER PLAY

Photography by Phil Inglis

BROADWAY BOOKS New York

BROADWAY

First published in the United States in 1996 by Broadway Books, a division of Bantam Doubleday Dell Publishing Group, Inc., 1540 Broadway, New York, NY 10036.

Produced by Roeder Publications Pte. Ltd.

Photography by Phil Inglis at the Duke's Course, St. Andrews, Scotland. Photographs on Pages 39, 42, 43 and 47 by Marlene Roeder.

Broadway Books titles may be purchased for business or promotional use or for special sales. For information, please write to : Special Markets Department, Bantam Doubleday Dell Publishing Group, Inc., 1540 Broadway, New York, NY 10036.

Library of Congress Cataloging-in-Publication Data

Player, Gary
Bunker Play / by Gary Player with Michael Wade. — 1st ed.
     p.   cm. — (The golf masters series)
ISBN 0-553-06940-3
1. Bunkers (Golf) 2. Sand traps. 3. Swing (Golf) 4. Wedge shot (Golf)   I. Wade, Michael.   II. Title. III. Series.
GV979.B86P53 1996
796.352'3—dc20   96-25431
                                                             CIP

FIRST EDITION

Printed in Singapore

ISBN 0-553-06940-3

96 97 98 99 00 10 9 8 7 6 5 4 3 2 1

CONTENTS

CONTENTS

THE ESSENTIAL
GARY PLAYER

How do you describe a living legend like Gary Player? Words like determined, superfit and courageous come to mind. As do phrases like "one of the all time golfing greats", or "the best bunker player in the world", or "the man in black", or occasionally "the toughest of competitors".

All these reflect some facets of the man, and they have been applied to him over the years by a great many of his peers and most commentators. But do they entirely sum up Gary Player?

It's true that his record of Championship wins is more than impressive. He is one of only four golfers to have won the modern Grand Slam (the others being Ben Hogan, Gene Sarazen and Jack Nicklaus). He won three British Opens in three decades over three of the most formidable courses: Royal Lytham, Carnoustie and Muirfield. He also won three Masters, two US PGAs and a US Open.

Then, joining the Seniors circuit in 1985, he completed what he calls a Senior Slam: the British Senior Open, and US Senior Players Championship, the US PGA Seniors and US Seniors Open. While winning these tournaments, and many others around the globe, his game has been almost as good as ever. In 1988, for example, his average score in the US was 70.41 per round and Gary later confessed that these were the happiest and most enjoyable days of his life.

It is just as well, because the continuing success (and the pleasure of traveling the world with his wife Vivienne) has kept him from his other great interest: breeding race horses. He has chosen to stay at home in South Africa rather than base himself in the US, and there he has successfully bred and raced horses, his ambition being to lead in a Derby winner. But for the Seniors, golf would have been the loser.

That Gary became the greatest bunker player in the world is not open to question. Time after time, under pressure in the closing holes of a tournament, often under the beady eye of the TV camera, he has splashed out from the sand for a tap in. Golfers around the globe remember those shots, as do his fellow competitors, usually ruefully.

This expertise was developed from unremitting practice. No golfer (except possibly Ben Hogan) has ever worked harder on his game and there are many apocryphal stories of the young Player spending hours in a practice bunker before being carried into the clubhouse, seized up, complaining that he still had to sink that third sand shot.

Gary's determination to stay superfit is also legendary. He always believed that a golfer is an athlete and should train his body accordingly. At 5 feet 7 inches, weighing 145 pounds, he had to be strong, with the stamina to match any of the power players. So he has long practiced a rigorous regime of running, weight lifting, gym workouts and even finger push ups that would daunt a modern Olympian. His diet too has been Spartan. Plenty of fruit, vegetables, nuts, wheat germ and water, unappealing to the average golfer, but it seems to keep Gary incredibly fit.

This stamina allied to the most competitive spirit in the game is what makes him a winner. Gary just never gives up. Whatever his position, he concentrates his utmost on his next shot until the very last hole. No other golfer has won more Championships coming from behind on the final holes than he has. His sheer determination to win is acknowledged, almost with awe, by all his peers.

Two examples underline his fighting qualities, in head-to-head match play and stroke play. In the final of the 1965 World Match Play Championship at Wentworth, Gary was six down after the morning round to "Champagne Tony" Lema. The stylish American, who was tragically killed in an air crash a year later, had won seven holes in a row "throwing super golf" at Gary, who could "only hang on for dear life".

Then Lema won the first hole of the afternoon round to go seven up - and it seemed all over. But this was a situation tailor-made for Gary's never-say-die attitude. He won three out of the next four with birdies and put the pressure on. Three down with six to play at the 13th hole, he then holed a crucial ten-foot putt for a win (after Lema had bottled in a 25-footer) and squared the match on the final hole. He then won the first extra hole with two clinical putts, after Lema had exploded from a deep greenside bunker way past the hole. The match was a thriller: a head-to-head never to be forgotten, the greatest match play contest to date.

Then, thirteen years later, Gary won a major in one of the greatest claw-backs in history. In the 1978 Masters, starting the final round seven shots behind Hubert Green and Tom Watson, he shot seven birdies over the last ten holes (around the notorious Amen corner) to win his third green jacket. Seve Ballesteros, who played with him on that historic final round, said later he believed that Gary had "willed himself to victory". It was a triumph of concentration and courage.

Those qualities are very evident in Gary Player. But there is also a third virtue that's a very important part of his personality, as I found out, namely "courtesy".

I had an appointment to meet Gary for the first time during the 1995 British Open at St. Andrews and arrived to see him lunching with family and friends in a hotel restaurant. He was tucking into a mixed salad and sipping mineral water (what else?). I was about to introduce myself when a gray-haired lady, clutching a large book, approached his table timorously, asking for an autograph. Now Gary must have been a little weary as he'd just finished the second round and there was a keen wind blowing across the course. But he got up from the table, greeted the lady warmly and stood talking to her for several minutes before she left, smiling. It was a kind gesture, typical of the man…and it has been a pleasure for me to work with him on this book.

As a postscript, if Gary had not qualified for the next two rounds we would have started to collaborate on the book the next day. Typically, of course, he made the cut….

Michael Wade

Michael Wade

Fundamentals

THE SWING

Most golfers dislike bunkers. After a long iron that just misses the green, they would rather find their ball buried calf-deep in clinging rough, it seems, than lying cleanly on the sand in a greenside trap. In such a bunker, they approach their ball warily. They don't want to be embarrassed by leaving it in the sand; they just want to get out, anywhere on the green, as quickly as possible. So they clamber down into the bunker, gazing at the flag, not taking in the state of the sand or the run of the green. First they dig their feet well in, as they have heard a good sand player should, but they still hold their club at the end of its shaft. Then they open the face of their sand wedge, having already gripped it firmly, by turning their hands and wrists a little clockwise. As often as not, they will then freeze into a stance, leaning right, as they feel the ball has to be hit up to clear the lip ahead. Finally, they make a quick swing, stabbing the wedge deep into the sand... .

No wonder they don't like bunkers. Very few have a clear idea of the basic fundamentals of sand play. Perhaps not one in a hundred has ever taken even one lesson from his club professional on the subject, yet nothing else would improve their game so immediately and drastically. For good bunker technique improves both the short game and the long, the long benefiting from the confidence that comes in knowing that playing from sand can be much easier than playing from deep rough.

Bunker shots have often had a major impact in winning a major championship. They are frequently spectacular, whether from fairway bunkers or greenside ones. Three examples, spanning more than 60 years, underline the importance of good sand play.

First there's Bobby Jones (who else?). In the 1926 British Open at Royal Lytham St. Annes, playing with Al Watrous neck and neck, he drew his tee shot at the 400-yard 71st hole. His ball ended in a shallow "waste" bunker, lying cleanly, some 170 yards from the flag, with sandhills in between. Bobby hit it 100 per cent clean from the sand with his mashie iron (almost the equivalent of a modern 4-iron) and it finished on the green closer to the hole than Al Watrous's ball. It was a tremendous shot and it rattled Watrous, who three-putted to Bobby's two putts. Bobby finally won the Open, finishing in 291 against 293 for Watrous. His mashie iron now reposes as "a sacred relic" in the Royal Lytham clubhouse, and a plaque marks the spot on the course where he played his historic sand shot.

Another American, Bob Tway, also played a spectacular sand shot to win the 1986 US PGA at Inverness, Ohio. "Partnering" Greg Norman, tied on the 72nd hole, Tway had put his ball into a greenside bunker on the front right-hand side of the green. Norman's ball was lying on the front edge of the green, up against the collar, but it seemed to be his advantage. Then Tway sank his splash shot and Norman, staggered, three-putted. Once again, at the death, a good sand shot had won a major.

Finally, there's the fairway bunker shot of Scotland's Sandy Lyle, which won him the 1988 Masters at Augusta. Once again, the drama took place at the end of the 72nd hole. Needing a par four to tie Mark Calcavecchia, Lyle hit one of the greatest pressure bunker shots, from the first bunker on the left, onto the green and sunk the putt to win the Championship (it's described in more detail on page 138). Yes, good sand play can certainly help you win at golf, from a major to a weekend match.

I am sure that my ability in playing from sand has been the most significant aspect of my game in every one of my 17 major championship victories on the regular and senior tours. Bunker shots are my favorite and when playing in a tournament I have always attacked the flag. If I have missed a green and landed in a bunker, I have always had complete confidence in getting "up and down" in two.

Such certainty is one reason I never get negative on the course. Confidence in sand play comes from knowing and understanding the fundamentals, applying them and honing them with thoughtful practice.

The Pre-Shot Routine

The basic fundamentals of sand play are best demonstrated by considering a standard ten-yard shot from a greenside bunker, where the ball is lying cleanly on top of firm sand. They apply to virtually all types of bunker shots, with certain key variations, depending on lie, distance, sand and weather conditions.

First, before you climb quickly down into the bunker and try to splash the ball out anywhere on the green, you have to think very positively and assess the situation carefully. You must be positive because you are really aiming to hole out from the bunker, not just knock the ball onto the green or close to the flag.

Think about it. If you were already on the green, ten yards from the hole, you would certainly try and hole your putt. You would also try to hole out

The Basic Bunker Shot

RIGHT: *For the standard bunker shot, stand wide and open, weight left, with your club face wide open.* CENTER RIGHT: *Swing back smoothly, with an early wrist cock.* BELOW CENTER RIGHT: *"Strike the match", hitting into the sand one and a half inches behind the ball.* FAR RIGHT: *The follow through will come naturally.*

your chip if you were chipping from the fringe at ten yards, so why not think the same from the sand? Aiming to just get close, say into a circle some six to ten feet in diameter around the hole, is not very positive. It's better than just trying to get out anywhere on the green and you would probably succeed in ending up somewhere in the circle. But if you aim to hole out, you'll finish closer still and you may well succeed on more than one occasion.

With this positive attitude, you must then assess your bunker shot just as you would a chip or a putt. When putting from this distance, you decide first just where you should aim to allow for breaks due to cross slopes and the grain of the grass. Having found your line, you then determine just how hard to stroke the putt. Is the green fast, or wet? Are you putting downhill, or up? You take all these observations into account before you settle down to your practice stroke.

The Basic Bunker Shot

Now you do exactly the same on a bunker shot. True, you can eliminate many of the breaks, as you aim to land the ball on a spot quite near the hole, from which it can roll in. But you need to look very closely at the area immediately around the hole itself.

If the flagstick doesn't lean as the cup is set upright, a check on the depth of soil around the hole can be revealing. More soil lies on the high side, indicating the severity of the slope. Check the grass around the hole carefully as well. If it's more worn on one side, that's the low side because more balls have rolled into it than the high. Dead blades of grass on one side of the hole should also be checked as they show that the grain runs across the hole in that direction so their roots have been cut when the green was mowed.

Having read the green around the hole and decided on the spot you should aim for from the bunker, you then have to read the sand. Now, I know we are considering a standard ten-yard shot from a good lie on firm sand, but you must make it a pre-shot routine to analyze every shot from any bunker, every time.

There is far more to read in a bunker than on any green in the world. In fact the most amount of reading, or assessment, that takes place in golf is in the bunker. The first thing to decide once you are standing in the bunker is the condition of the sand. How much of it is there beneath your feet and, if you're not playing on your home course, what type of sand is it?

If your home course has plenty of sand in the bunkers and the shot you are about to play is from a bunker with little sand and what there is of it is hard, then you have to hit your shot much easier. Otherwise the club will bounce up a little, the ball will come out too fast and fly over the green. The reverse applies if the bunker has more sand than you're used to - you'll have to make a longer swing than usual to get the necessary force.

You should also identify the sand, of which the four most common types are river, limestone, silica and coral. Each has very different playing characteristics (see pages 34 ff) which depend on grain size, source, particle distribution and weather factors. With high-purity silica sand, for example, shots rarely spin well.

Then you must read the possible effects that the way your ball is lying will have on the shot. Is it on an upslope or a down? Above your feet or below? If it's on a downslope it will come out low, so what's the height of the front lip? Is it lying, in fact, close under a lip, front, back or side, or in a rake mark? Rough soft sand and rake marks impose unfair penalties on the golfer, making it very difficult to recover. You can't get backspin if you're lying in a rake mark, which is why I'm against the use of rakes. It is far better to use a T-shaped length of ordinary pipe at the end of the handle, in place of the rake, and scrape the bunkers with that, or use the back of the rake if you wish.

You will also have to consider carefully how to play the shot if your ball is plugged in the sand with only its top showing in a "fried egg" lie, or if it has buried itself in its own pitch mark in soft sand. Then there is the effect of the weather. Is rain compressing the sand? Is the wind blowing strongly with you, or against you, or is it across your line of shot? A ball comes fairly softly out of a bunker and a strong cross-wind can affect its flight.

So there are many factors that need to be taken into account and you must do this as a pre-shot routine before you can address your ball. You determine just where on the green you will land the ball and you must try and visualize the swing you will make that puts it there, so that it lands precisely and rolls into the hole. While "seeing" the shot and judging the feel, I sometimes take a practice swing just outside the bunker, or sometimes I do it inside. But it's never a full swing. What I rehearse is the wristy takeaway, part of the fundamentals of good sand play.

Now you're almost ready to execute a good shot from the sand, landing it on the spot you've marked out on the green. Fortunately, in the ten-yard shot you're about to play, you have a good lie and the sand is firm. So be

positive. You do not have to change your swing in sand play. Apart from an earlier wrist cock and a slower rhythm, it should basically be the same, in terms of your usual swing plane, as that of say, your medium iron.

All top golfers swing their sand wedges as they do their medium irons, despite apparent differences in style. For example, my personal list of great sand players includes golfers like Bobby Locke, Julius Boros, Sam Snead, Chi Chi Rodriguez, Isao Aoki and Seve Ballesteros. Now you might think that they all seem to play their greenside bunker shots in completely different ways - Boros with a loose, almost floppy, action; Snead, long and ultra slow; Chi Chi, quick and firm; Aoki, seeming to almost chop the ball out - yet they all use the same type of swing in a bunker that they use in their long game.

There is no need for a fancy wrist break in the takeaway. Do not take the club back outside the line of your feet and shoulders and then pull it down across your body. Most of the important fundamental changes are made at address. Once you have set up right, you just go ahead and swing normally - and this applies regardless of the lie.

To appreciate these changes in the set-up, you have to understand the geometry of sand play, the first part of which concerns the club face. On most bunker shots this needs to be open to some degree. Open means that when you are holding the club in your usual grip, the shaft straight up beneath your hands, its bottom edge will not be square to the line of your shot. Rather it will be facing right of your target, the toe of the club having rotated a little clockwise.

The reason you need to do this is that opening the club face increases the effective loft of the sand wedge and allows its sole to slide more easily through the sand under the ball. Don't forget, this is the one shot in golf where you do not contact the ball with the club face. The ball is moved upward and forward by the sand beneath it.

The more open the sand wedge and the more "laid back" the club face is, the easier it will slide through the sand. This means it will "take" less sand, which should be a shallow cut of around half an inch depth, and the ball will fly higher. For a similar strength of shot, a square club face will slice through about an inch down, sending the ball out on a lower trajectory, while a closed club face will knife into the sand about one and a half inches, propelling the ball out on a low arc with topspin.

The ability to vary the degree you hold the club face open, which ultimately controls the flight of the ball, is one reason for not using a patent compound wedge with a built-up sole. This may help you to get out of the bunker every time with a standard shot, but you'll find it hard to vary length and height. The ride and the bounce of your sand wedge are important to stop the club from digging too deep into the sand (see details of equipment on pages 29 ff) but you must be in control of this for all shots.

So with a standard shot, where you are aiming to land your ball some eight yards away so it can roll into the hole, open the club face a little. Rotate the toe of the club to the right by some fifteen degrees, or about one and a half inches from a square position. This will allow you to see most of the face of the club, making it look a bit like a frying pan. Then, and only then, standing in the bunker above your ball with the club not grounded to avoid penalty, should you grip it firmly in your normal grip but an inch down from the top of the shaft, to make up for the depth you will dig your feet down into the sand at address. If you then set up square to your target line and swing through the sand however, the open club face would make the ball squirt off to the right. So you have to ensure that the geometry of your stance, the line of your feet and shoulders in other words, is also open to your target line. That means that you should turn your body to your left, with the line of your feet, hips and shoulders pointing well left of your target. When you come to swing, the club will follow your body alignment as it does with your normal swing using a mid iron.

As the line of your feet and shoulders is open to the target line in the bunker, you are swinging back across the target line and down through it, effectively putting cut spin on the ball with an open club face. The more open the club face and stance, the greater the spin and the higher and shorter the shot. Sometimes on a very delicate short shot, I will stand almost facing the target with the club face opened all the way. You should follow my example.

Now you need to build your stance in the bunker to play the standard shot, and it must be one that inhibits any body sway. One of the worst things you can do is stand too narrow, because if your feet are close together it results in a tendency to sway. Swaying is bad on any shot, but once you start swaying in a bunker, you never hit the same distance behind the ball consistently. So stand with your feet a little wider than in your normal stance. This also stops you from using your legs too much in the swing which inhibits any weight transfer and makes you use your hand more.

With the ball positioned just inside your left heel, you need to wriggle your feet well into the sand to ensure your stance is firm - you don't want any sinking down or slipping as you swing. You must also brace your right foot, so that its inside edge is lower than its outside one. The build-up of sand outside it will also help to prevent sway.

You should keep your weight more on your left foot than the right, in this case about 60 per cent on the left, as this will encourage you to cock your wrists earlier than with your normal swing. You have to take the club back steeply enough to clear the sand. Finally, with your body well braced but not locked stiff, you hover the head of your opened sand wedge above the sand about one and a half inches behind the ball. This is the point where it will enter the sand to slide through and emerge some two inches beyond the ball and you should focus your attention on that point rather than on the ball itself. As you would with a putt, check the area on the green you are aiming for and then look back at that point in the sand. You are now well set up for a good shot.

You are going to make a long, smooth, slow swing, one which only differs from your normal one in that it is slower and has an earlier wrist cock. It is also made with the hands and arms, with no body coil or weight transfer.

If you want to make a practice swing over the ball to judge the amount of force you put into the shot, do so. It's very difficult to advise on how hard you need to hit the ball to fly it eight yards. The feel for this comes from experience and practice. But as a rough guide, you might feel it requires twice the force you need for a pitch from a similar distance to allow for the resistance of the sand.

As for a forward press, or a trigger, for the swing - I don't use one. I just concentrate on keeping my arms and wrists lively and flexible. I "wobble" my wrists a little and waggle the club to keep some feeling of movement.

From the start of the takeaway, as you swing the club back along the line of your feet and shoulders, you must cock your wrists. The reason is that an early wrist cock is a bit like an elastic band. When you stretch one it snaps back automatically and with speed. If you go back stiff wristed, you'll never have any speed through the ball.

But let me explain exactly what I mean by a wrist cock, as many golfers seem to have strange ideas about what is involved. I do not cock my wrists by twisting my hands to the right, fanning the club face open, nor do I

Three Wedges

I always carry three wedges - a 60-degree and a 55-degree sand wedge and a pitching wedge to play all the different shots needed around the greens.

bend my hands down to the left. What happens is that my wrists give easily as the clubhead is swung back. When the club shaft is parallel to the ground and the line of my feet, and my hands have moved to a position opposite my right thigh, the back of my left hand is pointing forward. It is not pointing up to the sky, or down to the ground. By the time my arms are horizontal, the club shaft is pointing vertically upward, or a little beyond it. That's a full, early wrist cock.

So you swing back like this, using your hands, wrists and arms, and you swing slowly. A bunker shot should always be nice and slow. There's an old saying: "Swing it slow for the dough. Swing it fast and you won't last." You must swing slowly to avoid hitting down on the ball at a steep angle. If you do that on a fairway and the ground is hard, the club will bounce and you will top the ball. In a bunker the opposite happens. Since the sand is soft, if you come down at the ball fast and at a steep angle you dig deep, compress the sand and stay in the bunker.

How far back should you swing? Well, you need a long, full swing on all but very short shots. It will give you more time to gauge distance and gain that all-important feel, but you must guard against decelerating the club as you skim it through the sand, which is fatal.

At the top, the best way I can describe the downswing is to think of "striking the match". This implies a firm, crisp action. If you try and strike a match too hard, its head breaks off. If you decelerate the action and dab at the side of the box, the match doesn't light.

When golfers don't strike the match on the downswing, they decelerate. Their wrists roll over, the club face closes and they dig deep into the sand. This is something you want to avoid so strike the match, swing crisply through the sand and you will not have to think about releasing your wrists through impact as that will be automatic.

You don't have to think about the follow through either. A full follow through makes sure you don't decelerate or leave the club in the sand. But if you strike the match firmly, it will also be automatic. On a standard ten-yard shot from a good lie, your hands should end up about chest high.

And it was a good shot you've just played. You may not have holed it, but you got close enough for a tap in. So now you need to do it again. Remember, there's nothing like practice to build confidence, which is the key to good sand play. The fundamentals you've just reviewed can be applied to every bunker shot with just a few alterations.

I can't emphasize enough how important a sharp short game is for a golfer. Some 70 per cent of all golf shots are played from 60 yards in to the flag and a large percentage of these are sand shots. To underline this point, let's take a player with a 14 handicap and give him some help in the shape of two considerable players: John Daly and Corey Pavin.

If John Daly hit every drive for the 14 handicapper, who then took over to play the other shots in every hole, that handicapper would finish at say ten over par. But if the 14 handicapper hit every drive and every second shot and Corey Pavin played for him within 60 yards of the green, he would finish at about three over par. That's food for thought.

THE EQUIPMENT

Until the 1930s, sand play was a totally hit-and-miss affair for the average player. Not only were lies usually difficult as rakes were scarce, but the clubs used to extract the ball were very unsuitable. The niblick, the equivalent of a modern 8-iron, was usually employed, but it was a club with a sharp leading edge that cut deeply into the sand at the slightest opportunity, resulting in shots being wasted in bunkers and mounting frustration.

Around this time, Bernard Darwin, that most talented and informed writer on golf, even wrote of a certain matched set of irons that contained two niblicks: "the standard 8 for normal shots and the emergency 88 laid way back for the trick trap shots that experts get through deliberately regulating the angle of the face." Trick shots? Darwin noted that he had never carried two niblicks in his bag and never would. It took a real expert, and a lucky one at that, who could consistently get down in two from the sand using a niblick.

Then along came Gene Sarazen and bunker play suddenly changed out of all recognition. One of the all-time greats, Sarazen won the US Open in 1922 and retired from tournament play after the 1973 British Open at Troon, where he holed the lethal par three No. 8, the Postage Stamp, in one. During those 51 years, he won seven majors and hit arguably the most famous golf shot in history, a 4-wood at the 1935 Masters for an albatross to gain him a play-off that he subsequently won. He also invented the modern sand wedge.

In the winter of 1931, Sarazen, who had been very erratic in his bunker play, started to tinker with his niblick. As usual, his problems had been caused by burying his club too deeply in the sand and he decided he needed something to lift the club up as it swung through under the ball. He had watched ducks landing and taking off from a pond and noted that they got lift by angling the leading edge of their wings compared to the trailing edges. So he soldered some metal onto the sole of his wedge and then filed it to create an angle between the front edge of the club and the rear, the front sitting off the ground when the club was soled with the shaft upright. He got lift-off. The club no longer dug into the sand; instead it bounced through it.

Sarazen then won the 1932 British Open and credited his victory to the new club. With it, he said he could "stand up confidently to any trap shot, clean, half-buried or buried. It demands many hours of practice, but once mastered, it's the greatest stroke-saver in the game. I'm proud to have invented it."

So he should be. But sand wedges have developed quite a long way since then, although the basic principles remain the same. So what should a handicap player look for in an ideal sand wedge to suit his game today? There's quite a choice of types around.

The Angle of Bounce

The sand wedge and its close relative the pitching wedge differ from the other irons not just in terms of their length, weight and loft, but also specifically because they have the flanged sole and angle of bounce invented by Gene Sarazen. Both are about half an inch shorter than the 9-iron in shaft length and weigh quite a bit more. Typically, there is a quarter of an ounce increase in weight between consecutive irons up to the 9-iron (so that the 8 is a quarter of an ounce heavier than the 7, for example.) The wedges though, are normally at least an ounce heavier than the 9, with the sand wedge in most cases being even heavier than the pitching wedge.

As for loft, the angle of the club face to the vertical, a 9-iron would typically have a loft of some 47 degrees, while a pitching wedge has some 51 degrees and a sand wedge varies from 55 to 60 degrees. The real difference in their performance comes from the flange, or sole, of the wedges, which extends below the horizontal to create an angle of bounce.

Typically, a 9-iron will have the back edge of its sole slightly higher than its front or leading edge when the shaft is held vertically, creating an angle of about two degrees above the horizontal. This sole angle allows the iron to bite crisply into the turf after it has contacted the ball, creating backspin. In the wedges however, with the back edges of their soles lower than the leading edges, there is a bounce angle of the sole below the horizontal and this amount of bounce gives them their ability to ride along just below the surface of turf or sand without digging in too deep.

A pitching wedge usually has a bounce angle of between two and five degrees, while a sand wedge has between two and eleven degrees, as well as a more rounded leading edge to ensure it doesn't cut too deep into the sand

and lose too much clubhead speed in the process. These variations in bounce angle and differences in the width of soles provide wedges suitable for different types of sand or ground conditions.

Many sand wedges produced today have a very wide sole, a large area between the leading and trailing edges. As a result, in certain conditions, they don't take enough sand and instead end up getting too much of the ball, topping it or flying it over the green. However, if you are playing on a course which has loose, fluffy sand in its bunkers, this is the type of wedge you need. One that digs deeper won't move the ball forward very much at all. Conversely, if the bunkers on your home course are filled with hard packed sand, you need a wedge with a smaller bounce angle and a narrower sole. This will bite deeper into the compact resistance of the sand and give you control of your shots.

Three Wedges for Every Shot

I always carry three wedges: a 60-degree sand wedge, a 55-degree sand wedge and a pitching wedge. With this choice, I can play all the different shots I might need around the green. But what would I recommend for the handicap golfer? Well, I believe you should aim for a similar combination, for these are the clubs that will really help you to score better.

The first requirement of the wedge is that you should be able to control your shot consistently; to fly the ball the right height and distance and have it land softly on the green. To achieve this softness, some manufacturers came up with a unique alloy for the clubhead: aluminum bronze. It's a soft alloy with a melting point of some 1,100 degrees Fahrenheit (593 degrees Celcius), compared to the 1,500 degrees Fahrenheit (815 degrees Celcius) needed to melt stainless steel, making it some 30 per cent softer than stainless steel as a result. This characteristic, combined with a patented heat treatment process allows the clubheads to be made to the exact hardness necessary for feel and consistency.

As a result, the ball stays on the club face a fraction longer, which imparts more spin on the ball for better accuracy. The alloy heads also absorb vibration some 18 per cent more effectively than stainless steel when the clubhead meets the ball. Played correctly, the ball lands on the green as lightly as a feather.

The pitching wedge has 52 degrees of loft, a 3-degree bounce angle and a swing weight of D2. It can be very effective from the fairway, rough and

the chalk will mark the bottom of your club. If the marks are toward the toe, the club's too upright for your swing. If near the heel, it's too flat. He should then be able to arrange to alter the lie of your shafts quite easily, if necessary. Tournament professionals check their lie all the time when preparing for a championship since they know that this can make a big difference to scoring.

With all these factors, there is a great variety of sand wedges, or a combination of wedges, to suit every need. Whatever your needs for a sand wedge, think carefully about the club that will help you in the sand and make certain you choose well.

You often read in golf magazines about leading professional golfers extolling the virtues of a new driver with a high-tech shape, head, or shaft that gives them much greater length or accuracy. Others equally change their sponsors from time to time, finding all of a sudden that their new sponsor's irons are infinitely easier to play and considerably more accurate than their old ones. As for putters, certain pros seem to change them as often as they change their golf gloves. But for wedges, particularly sand wedges, that's a different story.

Once a pro finds a wedge that really suits him, he hangs on to it, even if he changes all the other irons in his bag. He practices with it constantly and develops considerable confidence in it, and his ability to use it, under the most difficult conditions. So should you.

Gene Sarazen demonstrated this belief perfectly at the 18th hole in the last round of the 1932 US Open, which was played at Fresh Meadow. He had pushed his approach shot into the treacherous bunker guarding the right of the green and enthusiastic spectators were clambering about everywhere, behind him and all around the fringe. As he was climbing down onto the sand, Paul Gallico, the sports writer, called out for him to wait until the crowd had been moved back. "Don't worry," Sarazen called back, "I'm not playing this shot. My sand iron is. It'll take care of me." It did. He splashed out to eight feet from the hole and sank the putt to win by three shots.

Now that's the sort of confidence you need to have for the club that will be your best friend in the sand!

and lose too much clubhead speed in the process. These variations in bounce angle and differences in the width of soles provide wedges suitable for different types of sand or ground conditions.

Many sand wedges produced today have a very wide sole, a large area between the leading and trailing edges. As a result, in certain conditions, they don't take enough sand and instead end up getting too much of the ball, topping it or flying it over the green. However, if you are playing on a course which has loose, fluffy sand in its bunkers, this is the type of wedge you need. One that digs deeper won't move the ball forward very much at all. Conversely, if the bunkers on your home course are filled with hard packed sand, you need a wedge with a smaller bounce angle and a narrower sole. This will bite deeper into the compact resistance of the sand and give you control of your shots.

Three Wedges for Every Shot

I always carry three wedges: a 60-degree sand wedge, a 55-degree sand wedge and a pitching wedge. With this choice, I can play all the different shots I might need around the green. But what would I recommend for the handicap golfer? Well, I believe you should aim for a similar combination, for these are the clubs that will really help you to score better.

The first requirement of the wedge is that you should be able to control your shot consistently; to fly the ball the right height and distance and have it land softly on the green. To achieve this softness, some manufacturers came up with a unique alloy for the clubhead: aluminum bronze. It's a soft alloy with a melting point of some 1,100 degrees Fahrenheit (593 degrees Celcius), compared to the 1,500 degrees Fahrenheit (815 degrees Celcius) needed to melt stainless steel, making it some 30 per cent softer than stainless steel as a result. This characteristic, combined with a patented heat treatment process allows the clubheads to be made to the exact hardness necessary for feel and consistency.

As a result, the ball stays on the club face a fraction longer, which imparts more spin on the ball for better accuracy. The alloy heads also absorb vibration some 18 per cent more effectively than stainless steel when the clubhead meets the ball. Played correctly, the ball lands on the green as lightly as a feather.

The pitching wedge has 52 degrees of loft, a 3-degree bounce angle and a swing weight of D2. It can be very effective from the fairway, rough and wet sand and its full shot distance is between 80 to 110 yards. The sand wedge, which has 55 degrees of loft and 11 degrees of bounce, swing weight D6, can equally be used for a fairway approach shot of between 60 to 90 yards. It is also very useful for getting out of thick rough and for all types of sand play. Finally the wedge with 60 degrees of loft and an 11-degree bounce angle is very efficient from the fairway, rough and sand, and can be used to play finesse lob shots. Its maximum shot distance is 70 yards.

To help the high handicapper with his short game, some companies also produce an equivalent range of oversized wedges. Being some 10 per cent larger than traditional wedges, they have an enlarged hitting area and sweet spot as well as true cavity backs.

Aside from degrees of loft or bounce, another angle that is often totally ignored, or completely misunderstood, by handicap golfers is the lie of their clubs. It is very important. The lie is the angle between the shaft and the clubhead when the club is soled flat, and it can certainly affect the direction and the quality of every golf shot. The flatter the lie, the greater the angle of the club shaft from the vertical.

Everyone has an individual swing and a natural plane of swing, which can vary between very upright and very flat. This depends on how tall you are, the length of your arms and the way you stand to the ball at address.

The reason is that a tall golfer, who stands close to the ball and swings fairly upright, say by a degree or two, needs clubs with a one or two degree upright lie. If this is the case, the sole of the club will bite evenly into the turf at impact, with no twist, producing the shot he has planned. If, however, he has a club with a lie that is one degree flat, its toe will dig into the ground first as it comes into the ball. As a result, the heel of the club will pivot around the toe, opening the club face and causing the ball to slice or push out to the right.

Conversely, a golfer who swings one degree flat will find trouble using a club with a one degree upright lie. In this case, the heel of the club catches the ground first, pivoting the toe of the club around it. The club face closes and the result is a hook or a pull to the left. So you see, it's important to match the lie of your clubs to your individual swing.

How can you check this? Well, your club professional should be able to advise you. He could well have a lie board, a plank of wood with a band of chalk on it. After you've taken several swings at an imaginary ball on it,

Sand Traps

HAZARDS

The Rules of Golf classify only two areas on the course as hazards: bunkers and water. Of course, for the player there are many other worrying situations to cope with: trees, gorse, sloping lies and thick rough are all to be avoided, if possible.

Good golf course designers blend all these factors into making every hole a real challenge, although most holes look far more difficult than they really are. All types of features are used creatively to pose a series of problems for the golfer, and generally the easier the shot the golfer has to play, the harder the challenges facing him and vice versa.

For example, on a long par three, demanding a big carry over gorse and heather, the green would probably only be guarded by a single wide bunker set to one side. On a short par three, however, where you have a good lie and can also place your ball wherever you like on the tee, the green could well be quite small and ringed with deep pot bunkers on the side and water in front.

With the same thinking, on short par fours, where you are faced with a relatively easy approach shot to the green, you would find that the landing area for your drive is not all that large. The fairway may well have been narrowed by trees, a creek or strategically placed bunkers, which are designed to upset the golfer's equanimity and penalize him for any resulting poor shot.

Your lie, stance and angle of approach to the flag could also pose problems, as there are often slopes all around the landing area. This doesn't mean that the green is unguarded, far from it, but these are the typical challenges you face on easy par fours.

On a long par four however, you should expect things to be a little easier. As your approach shot will require a long iron or a fairway wood, clubs that the amateur golfer finds much more difficult to handle, you could expect the landing area for your drive to be relatively wide and flat, although it will still demand a well-struck shot. The surroundings of the green should also be fairly easy, with light rough from which you could pitch or chip positively and no deep bunkers to cause despair. The green however, could be something else again, with its surface covered with tricky contours and sloping ominously.

All these features are what make golf such a fascinating game. If you have few problems on a course, it becomes bland and boring. Understanding the problems posed on each hole helps you to play better. Realizing where the real trouble lies and avoiding it to the best of your ability is the key to a good score. But you must appreciate that many apparent trouble areas are illusionary: tall trees down a fairway often appear closer than they really are; so do some fairway bunkers, which lure you into playing away from them to be trapped by deep rough on the other side, while a lake running alongside a hole makes judgment of distance very hard indeed.

Leaving aside golfers' personal pet hates (some hate being in the woods, or having to carry over a high tree, while others flinch from driving over a rocky chasm, or having to carry over a deep swathe of heather, or flirt with a long out-of-bounds), let's look at the most important hazard you will find on most courses: the sand. Never mind the water. If your ball plunges into a lake or a creek, that's it. You take your penalty without any option, unless by a million to one chance you happen to be lying an inch or so deep on the edge where you could try a very risky shot.

Bunkers, however, can be very different. Certainly there are those bunkers which cause more penalty shots than water, but many others can be a preferred option, better than finding your ball buried in heavy rough, rocks, creeks or a thick copse of trees. Most of them can positively help a golfer play his way around the course, provided he understands just why they are placed where they are and what it is they highlight.

Types of Sand

Bunkers first developed in the early days of golf quite naturally. The links courses had sand lying just beneath the close cropped turf which, being public land, was grazed by sheep. As these animals scraped for salt, or huddled together in hollows beneath the icy winds, patches of sandy ground appeared all over the course. Rabbits were also responsible for digging out a few deep scrapes, which contributed to the general hazards.

Before the invention of the sand wedge by Gene Sarazen and before bunkers were raked as a matter of course, getting out of the sand wasn't easy. Even today most golfers think of sand as a soft, unpredictable surface, which frustrates their efforts at all times just to get onto terra firma, never mind advancing farther towards the flag. But sand itself has several important factors that should be appreciated, if you want to play at your best.

Saving and Collection Bunkers

OPPOSITE: *Three saving bunkers on the left and a face bunker in front of the flag protect the 1st hole of Gleneagles' King's Course in Scotland.*
BELOW: *A deep collection bunker guards the left flank of the green on the 8th hole at Royal Troon.*

In the first place, all sand is silica (SiO_2) but its composition varies to a certain degree all over the world and almost all golf courses use the "natural" sand found in their location. In the tropics, many golf courses have bunkers filled with coral sand, which contains a fair amount of shell in it. As a result, the grains are quite large and pack together loosely. When a ball lands in one of these bunkers, it will tend to sit up on top of the sand and can be played out without problem.

Sand made out of limestone, which is found on inland tropic courses, is quite similar in allowing you to play out with backspin and control, unless it's ground too finely in which case it tends to produce buried lies, from which you cannot get backspin.

While local sand is usually used to save cost, some golf course designers specify very white sand for aesthetic reasons. This very pure silica sand is often imported from Idaho in the USA or comes from Australia. While the bunkers may provide a beautiful contrast with the rich green fairways, the sand grains are too rounded and mobile, so your ball will tend to sit down well in them and you're not likely to get any control when you blast out.

Fortunately for golfers worldwide, the most common type of sand found in bunkers is river, pit or beach sand. This tends to have hard, gritty grains on which the ball sits up well. Some river sands however can be contaminated with silt, which will cause it to set like concrete when wet. Too much of a shell content will attract worms on inland courses. Beach sand is often too fine and in St. Andrews, the home of golf, sand for the bunkers is carefully taken from a particular part of the beach where it is just coarse enough.

The most important factor about sand is the shape of its grain, and this comes in eight different grades of granulation. Pit or quarry sand has very angular grains which tend to bind tightly together, but some sea sand is too rounded and as a result too mobile. Very fine sand is also a pain as it blows out of the bunkers on windy courses and often sets with a "crust" in certain conditions, proving an unfair hazard.

Coarse, rounded sands on the other hand allow the ball to plug excessively and offer an unstable footing. The ideal composition is a medium grade of sand, of some 2.5 mm in size, and semi-rounded. This gives a firm surface, from which water will drain away well and you can play off in most circumstances with confidence.

Bunkers by Design

If bunkers were originally created in the old days by rabbits and sheep, today they are most certainly designed into courses with a great deal of care. Apart from being carefully placed to encourage the well-struck shot or to unnerve the fainthearted, they should also clearly indicate the best way to play a particular hole and highlight certain danger areas.

Unfortunately, some modern courses sport some large, very flat fairway bunkers, which are so shallow you could take a driver to play out of them. They are shallow largely to cut down costs, but they are not what bunkers are all about. Another dreadful trend places bunkers too close to the surface of a green. This is purgatory for greenkeepers, as sand is always splashed onto the putting surface, causing damage and disease to the grass. If the sand is made up of coarse particles and has a high lime content, it will be incompatible with the top dressing material. In any case, it will cover up the turf, which leads to mould and in the long run weakens the turf itself.

Sand should also not be placed too close to the putting surface, as that is rarely a fair hazard for the golfer. On a good course you should be able to use your putter from the immediate surroundings of the green.

Overall from fairway to green, there are three different types of bunkers that positively aid the golfer in playing the hole, namely directional, carry and saving bunkers. Two other types, called definition and face bunkers, can be both a help or a difficult hazard, while waste, collection and pot bunkers come under the dangerous hazard classification and should be avoided at all cost.

Directional bunkers are designed to help by indicating the best route or direction for your drive. They are usually placed well down the fairway on par fours or fives, way out of reach of the handicap player, even if he hits his Sunday best shot. You should aim directly at them, because that will keep you clear of trouble on the other side of the fairway. This strategy will often open up a dog-leg for you and certainly give the best line of approach to the green.

Carry bunkers, so called because they threaten the landing area of your drive so that you must carry them, can help to define that area more clearly, although they often inhibit a free swing by their mere presence. You should not be too concerned. They are usually placed well short of your optimum landing area, but if you do catch your ball a little thin and find yourself in the sand, the chances are you'll be in a good lie as these bunkers are usually fairly large and flat.

The third helpful bunker type is the saving bunker, which is usually found around the green. This type invariably indicates real trouble spots, as the bunkers are carefully positioned to stop the ball from bouncing or rolling down into them. A steep slope leading to an out-of-bounds to the right of the green will sometimes be marked by a saving bunker above it, which will grab an over-hit approach shot or slice.

You often find them behind a green, blocking the way to water or trees. As they almost invariably give you an uphill lie, recovery onto the green is rarely difficult; the option is certainly better than from the trouble they bar. So you can usually play positively at the flag.

If saving bunkers help to define trouble areas, definition bunkers are positioned to outline the target area for your drive off the tee, or to help you judge your line or the distance to the flag. By far the most common type of bunker on any course, the fairway version will pose more difficult problems, due to steepness of front slope or lie, on the shorter par fours.

The greenside hazards, when viewed in relation to the flag, should give some indication of how much green there is between hole and bunker, which helps in club selection. Sometimes these bunkers, which can bracket the green, are deep and difficult to escape from, so you should never flirt with them.

Face bunkers, which are found in front of the green more often than not, can help to decide the area of green you should play for. But they are often positioned to mask the distance to the flag from the edges of the putting surface. They show their front face (or faces, as some are quite large and kidney-shaped) to the approach shot and this can be quite steep. If they are also deep, with a sharp down slope in front, you should take care to play well clear of them.

Great care is also needed with waste bunkers, which come in the menacing hazard category. Usually long, flat areas of sand surrounded by local shrub rather than fairway grass, they often feature clumps or islands of grass inside them to create an even more difficult problem for the golfer. Sometimes you can get lucky with your lie and pick your ball cleanly off the sand or if you're close to the green, play a standard splash shot.

Waste, Collection and Definition Bunkers

OVERLEAF, LEFT: *A waste wilderness should be avoided on the 4th hole of the Quarry Course at Joondalup in Western Australia.* TOP RIGHT: *A wide collection bunker, set to catch all but the best struck shots, lies below the green at the Quarry Course's 2nd hole.* BELOW RIGHT: *Saving bunkers define the edges of the 2nd fairway of the Dunes Course at Joondalup.*

However, you should aim to stay well clear, as you can never be sure just how good a lie you'll get. For this reason, you should also avoid waste areas whatever you do. These are technically not hazards, but resemble waste bunkers choked with even more shrub and often clusters of rocks. If you're unlucky enough to find yourself in one, just aim for the nearest patch of fairway and get out in one if you possibly can.

Another type of dangerous bunker, mostly found lining the fairways of older courses, often on the inside corner of a dog-leg, is the gathering, or collection, bunker. These are designed to catch all but the best struck tee shot, as most of the surrounding fairway slopes into them. They can be small and deep, or large and deep, but in almost all cases, they have a high face of 1:1 or steeper.

A classic example is found in front of the 17th green, the "Road Hole", at St. Andrews. It swallows up every short approach and even short pitches and putts stroked along the narrow green, as Japanese golfer Tommy Nakajima found out to his cost in the 1978 British Open. He unwittingly putted into it and eventually emerged shaken with a nine on his card.

You should most certainly take good note of these score-wreckers, mark them carefully on your chart of the course and think hard before you play any shot in their general direction. If you're unlucky enough to be gathered up by one though, you will generally not have any options. You can forget about hitting toward the green; you just have to play out. You will just have to swallow the medicine and make certain you get out in one.

Much the same thinking applies to pot bunkers, which are small, round and deep, with steep faces everywhere that demand a high recovery shot. However, they are sometimes so difficult that they might force a handicap golfer to take an unplayable lie, as in one of the most notorious, which lurks at the edge of the 10th green at Pine Valley. Pot bunkers are probably the most menacing form of the hazard and provide a real challenge for you to keep calm in their vicinity and just play steadily on toward the flag.

Strategy

Once you start to understand bunkers, your attitude toward them will change. Before you play any hole, you should start to think hard about its defenses, real or imaginary, and the bunkers in particular. First of all, especially if the course is new to you, get a feel for the sand, which you can judge from a practice bunker usually by walking in it and scrunching your feet down. Note what type the sand is, how soft or well-packed down and try to estimate the effect it will have on your shots if you find yourself buried in it.

Second, realize just why the bunkers are positioned exactly where they are on every hole. Note the ones you can play toward, those you have to flirt with and the ones you must avoid. Sometimes you have to play to an area guarded or framed by fairway bunkers, which are placed to narrow the landing area, so you may not have an option.

But you should not get too greedy in these cases, as you certainly shouldn't when faced by a cross pattern of carry bunkers stretching diagonally across the fairway, or a cluster of them guarding a dog-leg and inviting you to try a little too hard on your approach. Just don't risk too much, as you don't want to face too tough a recovery.

If you try to understand them, bunkers can really help you score better by revealing how best to tackle any hole. This will help you gain confidence, particularly if you practice your sand shots, even taking a lesson or two on them from your local professional. Most pros, in fact, will tell you that they prefer to find themselves in a bunker rather than in deep rough, because they can generally control the ball much better from the sand.

Confidence is everything in golf. It comes from understanding the terrain and the techniques, from practicing thoughtfully on and off the course and, above all, from a positive mental attitude. Golf is very much a game of the mind. You have to contend with the course, the weather, frustration, stress and luck - the "rubs of the green". You can't combat luck, but you most certainly can control yourself and develop a positive mental attitude.

You must think positively. If you see yourself as an unlucky golfer, if you're sure you'll get a bad bounce off your drive and roll into a bunker or plunge into the water, then you will. But if you keep telling yourself that you can drive long and straight, chip like a wizard and putt like a champion, then you have a head start on the whole thing. What you think, you will be. If you think defensively, you will play negatively. Think positive and you will play positively.

You must never, never brood on past failures. If on the first tee of your home course, you think for a second that you usually hit your drive into the deep rough to the right of the fairway bunker, be sure you will. How much better to remember the summer when the ground was hard and you drove your ball into the throat of the green. That's the way to play.

Hidden Bunkers

OPPOSITE: *The gorse-lined fairway of the 4th hole at St. Andrews' Old Course looks wide and trouble-free....BELOW: But a deep-pot bunker lurks in wait by the green.*

Ban every negative thought from your mind and every memory of a bad shot. Instead, concentrate only on the good ones. Draw up a success list of all the very best shots you have ever hit on each of the holes you are about to play. Remember the time you nearly holed in one on the short 7th, or when your bunker shot from beside the green brought you a par at the most difficult 10th, or when the putt you sank two weeks ago on the 18th won you the match. That's the way to tackle the course.

I am sure that positive thinking has helped me win many matches and even some majors. The 1978 Masters at Augusta was one in particular. I started the last round seven shots behind Hubert Green, the tournament leader. Not much hope? I believe I willed myself to win.

I was playing with Seve Ballesteros and when we reached the vast gallery of people surrounding the 13th green I pointed to them and said to him: "They don't think I can win. But you watch, I'll show them". At that stage I was very focused and confident, steadily closing the gap at the top. In the end, I shot seven birdies over the last ten holes to win my third Masters, showing the real power of positive thinking.

Total concentration is very important. On the course, you must make every shot count. Don't think about the last one you played; focus only on the one you have to make, the one now. Analyze the target area, the lie, the wind - and then think about your club selection carefully. Go through your pre-shot routine every time, checking your grip, alignment and stance. Visualize the shot you will play: see the ball soaring off, reaching its peak, then dropping slowly onto the green. Then concentrate on the real shot. Look at the ball, focus on its logo ... and put your best swing on it.

Within this calm concentration, you have to play with certain courage, but you must also be well aware of your own capabilities. It's no good trying to take on a carry of 250 yards if your best effort off the tee usually only ends at 240. But there are also times when it is worth taking a calculated risk. You must assess each one as objectively as you can and always play the percentage shot if you're in any doubt.

When you think positively, visualizing a good shot is an important factor in pulling it off. It helps you to focus on a positive result rather than on the execution. So don't think how, think where. It's a bit like skimming a flat stone over the surface of a pond. When you do that you simply pick up the stone, look at the surface of the water and just skim it, hoping and expecting to get seven, eight or nine bounces.

focused on one shot at a time, playing the course, never the man. He also said that at least 20 per cent of all golf shots are largely a matter of luck, which tends to even out over a match.

This blithe approach is one to be copied. If your drive kicks hard right into a deep collection bunker or hits a branch and bounces out of bounds, don't grumble at your luck. You must try to be philosophical. Everyone playing the course has the same bad breaks sooner or later. And you might get a few good breaks before long. Bad breaks, or bad shots even, shouldn't rattle you.

I reckon a scratch player can expect to hit only some five good shots per round. These will probably be two close chips, a holed bunker shot and two sneaky putts. He would then probably make five errors, or have five bad breaks, to stay at par. As a handicap golfer, you have the right to make many more, so treat each one with indifference and just concentrate on the shot to come.

So determine that from now on you will no longer be the type of golfer that always carries his bunkers along with him. Make a positive effort to change your mental outlook, for you have nothing to lose but your fear of the sand and you have everything to gain in playing with more confidence.

You don't think about how you balance yourself, how your right arm folds, how you cock your wrist. As you throw the stone, you don't think about the role of your legs in the action, or how your right hand flicked through to give a smooth, swift throw. It must be the same with your next golf shot. Concentrate on just how it will fly and where it will end up. That will stop you brooding on how you are swinging the club - and believe me if you can achieve that on all shots your game will certainly improve!

Now relaxation and concentration might seem to be opposites, but this isn't so in golf. To be clearly focused, you must be mentally and physically relaxed, not tense or stressed. It should start even before you reach the first tee. Driving up late to the golf club, dashing into the locker room, rushing to meet your partners at the first with your shoe laces untied, without even a few practice putts, sets you back several shots a round. You will swing faster than normal, mis-hit the ball and probably lose your temper for good.

A comfortable approach to the game and a relaxed pace on the course helps you to maintain your rhythm and tempo. But you have to fight frustration and stress. It's easy to get very stressed on the golf course: a long, straight drive lands in a divot, you fluff a chip from light rough, or someone coughs as you're striking one of those putts ... and the next thing you feel like doing is throwing your clubs away and walking home.

One of the world's greatest practitioners in the art of staying relaxed was Bobby Locke, and many have a great deal to learn from his example. He was ultra-competitive and ultra-relaxed as well. Locke had just two speeds for everything he did in golf: leisurely and slow. He dressed carefully in the locker room, tying his shoelaces with the studied precision of a neuro-surgeon at work.

At the first tee, he ensured his score card was correct and pencils were sharp, and he then selected his club and ball with great deliberation. On the course, he moved with the stateliness of a bishop and invariably drove his playing partners, including myself, to utter distraction. Nothing would induce him to hurry, not even when he moved up to collect the trophy!

Now I am not advocating slow play, but I do believe that keeping relaxed and unflustered while you swing is important. Locke's record of four British Opens between 1949 and 1957 is testimony to that. He also firmly believed in concentration and luck as essential elements of the game. He

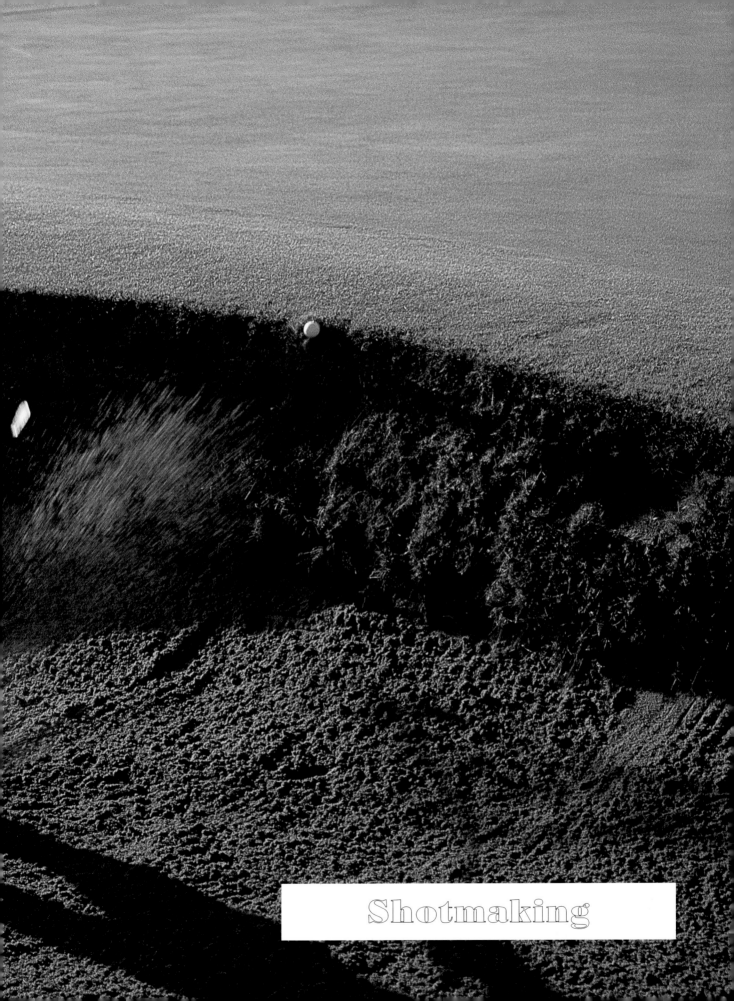

Shotmaking

AROUND THE GREEN

The standard shot from a good lie is often called the splash shot because it is played with feeling; gently, yet firmly, without the sheer force used in an "explosion" shot from a difficult lie. Summarizing its basic fundamentals, you dig your feet in, bracing the right, open your stance, keep your weight left, cock your wrists early and swing back slow, then strike the match, splashing through the sand under your ball.

Once you have mastered it through practice, you will have a reliable general purpose bunker shot in our bag. You will also be well on your way to coping with the most difficult sand saves. The same simple action is used in every type of bunker shot you play around the green, with certain variations in your set-up. From short shots of a few yards to long ones of 40 yards plus, from high shots with no spin to low shots with plenty of bite: you only need to understand how to adapt the basic shot to gain real confidence in the sand.

The 5-Yard Shot

From a good lie in the sand, the shorter the shot you wish to play the more you open your stance and your club face. For a shot to a flag just over the front lip of a bunker, say with only four or five yards of green to play with, I stand so open that my body almost faces the target landing area, with the club face as open as possible.

I grip the club with my left hand in its usual position, but with my right hand strengthened a little, turned more to the right, so that it is under the left through impact. I still play the ball off the left heel, with my weight on my left side and plan to enter the sand about one and a half inches behind it. The takeaway has the same tempo, the wrists cock quickly and the backswing is full. It's hard to time a shot with a short swing, although you must guard against decelerating the club from a full one. So you have to strike the match firmly.

The set-up creates an abrupt up and down, almost V-shaped, swing arc, which gets the ball up quickly. The position of the right hand allows it to flip under the left through impact, which farther increases the loft of the club and holds the club face open. This action means that your club face goes through the ball slightly ahead of your hands and there will be a concave break in the back of your left wrist through impact.

There are two points to bear in mind. If you haven't practiced this shot, swinging with a wide open club face often results in you hitting the ball with the hosel or the neck of the club, driving it deep into the bunker face. So when you practice it at first, try addressing the ball more off the toe of your sand wedge rather than in the center of the club face. You also have to remember that your ultra-open stance and club face will put a lot of cut, or slice, spin on the ball. On a level green, it will spin to the right on landing; something to think about when you're picking your target spot.

The High Shot without Spin

A high, short bunker shot has a very similar V-shaped action, although there is little spin on landing. You sometimes need to play this shot when you're in a deep greenside bunker and there is only a little green between you and the flag.

To play this shot successfully, you need to set up with the ball even more forward toward the left foot. You still maintain a wide stance, but this time you should set much of your weight on your right foot. Position your hands slightly behind the ball, with your right hand turned well to the right, as you are aiming for an even earlier flip action through impact.

Enter the sand farther behind the ball than for the standard shot, about two and a half inches behind. The extra sand between ball and club face means you will not get any backspin, just a high flying ball that drops gently on the green and stays put. Then when you've set up correctly, you just swing back smoothly and strike the match.

I was faced with just such a shot in the Japan Airlines Open at Chiba in 1972. I needed to par the 18th to win the tournament, but my approach to the green had landed in a deep and wet bunker. My shot from the sand ended up under three feet from the flag and I made the par to win by one shot. Up to then, it was the most difficult par I ever had to make to win, but the right technique saw me through.

The Low, Spinning Shot

The low bunker shot that bites on the green is also a very good one to have in your bag. Again, it is all made in the set-up, which is almost the opposite

OVERLEAF, TOP LEFT: *Open your stance so that your body faces the target landing area. Open the club face as well and as far as possible. Play the ball off your left heel, with your weight on your left side. Cock your wrists quickly.* TOP RIGHT: *Make a full backswing.* BELOW LEFT: *"Strike the match firmly."* BELOW RIGHT: *Your right hand will flip under the left through impact, increasing the loft of the club.*

to that used for the high shot, although, still just a variation of your standard one.

For starters, you must play the ball off the center of your stance. Your weight is on your left side as usual and your hands, with your normal grip, are slightly ahead of the ball. You do not set up very open; the club face has to be just open from square. You also stand closer to the ball and you aim to hit into the sand closer to the ball, perhaps half an inch behind it.

Delofting your sand wedge - by opening it very little - results in the ball coming out lower. Hitting closer behind it means you will have less sand between ball and club face, so you will get more spin. The ball should land on the green, take one bounce and then grip firmly.

This is not a shot you can play at St. Andrews with its deep pot bunkers. You can't play it with a big face in front of you at all and you usually consider the shot when you're in a flat greenside bunker and the flag is some twenty yards away. But with practice and feel it can be played very usefully over shorter distances, as I did on the 16th hole at Lytham St. Annes in the 1974 British Open.

It was one of the best bunker shots I have ever hit. Playing with Johnny Miller, I put my approach shot in a bunker on the left side of the green. The flag was on the extreme left hand side as well and I only had about nine feet of green, with a bank or slope between the bunker and the hole.

When I read the sand and read the green, I realized that if I pitched the ball out and landed it on the green over the slope it would probably have run some twelve feet past the hole. If I played it short and soft onto the bank there was a danger the slope would have killed it, with the ball rolling back into the bunker. So I decided to play a low shot with spin, aiming to land it on the slope and have it bounce forward toward the hole and then let it bite.

I took my sand wedge, opened the face a fraction, aimed an inch behind and landed the ball on the bank. It took one bounce and stopped three inches from the hole. Johnny Miller came up to me and said it was one of the best bunker shots he had ever seen. He still remembers it. Today whenever I see him he says: "How about that bunker shot you played on the 16th?"

The Shot with the Putter

FAR LEFT: *Set up with the ball in the back of your stance to prevent the ball from jumping straight up in the air and coming down as quickly.* LEFT: *Take the putter back as you would if you were on the green and treat the whole shot like a long putt. The length of the backswing determines the length of the shot.* BELOW FAR LEFT: *"Strike the match" with authority so that you don't leave the ball in the bunker.* BELOW LEFT: *If you have kept the putting stroke smooth and the follow through long enough, the ball will roll onto the green.*

The High Shot without Spin

OVERLEAF, TOP LEFT: *Your stance and club face should be well open and your weight on the right foot.* BELOW LEFT: *Turn the right hand a little to the right, so that it is under the left at impact.* RIGHT: *Cut through the sand two and a half inches behind the ball.* FAR RIGHT: *The ball will land softly, with little spin.*

The Low, Running Shot

I would play a run up if I had a lot of green to play with and the flag was up on a plateau. You don't want to pitch directly on the plateau, because you could probably find it very difficult to stop your ball rolling off the green into deep trouble.

So you judge your landing spot and the amount of run you need and play the ball off the center of your stance, with your weight left and your hands slightly ahead of the ball. The technique is similar to that required for the low, spinning shot. Only this time, you use your pitching wedge instead of your sand wedge.

Open your stance and your club face just a little. This in effect delofts the pitching wedge and, as a consequence, the ball will fly out low. Stand closer to the ball and you aim to hit into the sand about half an inch behind the ball. If you did this with your sand wedge, the ball would bite, but the loft of the pitching wedge will send it running on landing on the green.

The 45-Yard Shot

Long greenside bunker shots of up to fifty yards from sand to flag are some of the most exacting shots in golf. Although they are relatively uncommon, they can ruin a good score if you don't know what you're doing. If you do know, they can help you win matches or competitions and they've helped me win tournaments on several occasions.

One that's been talked about was the shot I played in the 1961 Sunshine Open at Bayshore, Miami Beach. After three rounds, I was tied in the lead with Julius Boros on 204, with Arnold Palmer four shots behind. Then Palmer made his customary last round charge, while I dropped shots, culminating at the 16th and 17th where I three-putted and overshot the green entirely.

I finally needed a birdie at the par five 18th to beat Palmer by one shot, but my second caught a bunker, the ball ending up fifty yards from the flag. I played one of the best long sand shots of my life, to within six feet of the flag, and sank the putt for the birdie and a winning score of 273. The papers called this the "trap shot win".

To play a longer bunker shot, say around twenty yards, you need to stand less open, with your club face only slightly open. Your weight is forward on your left foot and your hands must be slightly ahead of the ball. But you play this off the center of your stance and you aim to enter the sand closer to the ball, say about three-quarters of an inch behind. The set-up gives you more of a U-shaped swing arc, a flatter one through the sand, which drives the ball more forward.

On takeaway, you still cock your wrists early as with the standard shot and you swing back slow. But at impact, with your left hand going through ahead of the ball, your left wrist has a convex bend. This action takes loft off the club, so that the ball flies lower, with a "skip and bite" action, as you've entered the sand that much closer.

This same technique serves you well for all long bunker shots, but what do you do for thirty and forty yarders? The answer is that, as with a low running shot, you take another club. Faced with a thirty-yard bunker shot, you have to use your pitching wedge, not your 60-degree sand wedge. When you are forty yards from the hole, you use your 9-iron.

The best bunker shot I played in 1995 was with a 9-iron. It was in the US Seniors Open at Fort Worth. I found the sand at the 17th, some fifty yards from the flag and I took a 9-iron and nearly holed the shot. The ball ended up one inch away.

One last observation on long bunker shots, in fact on all bunker shots: no matter what the lie, the average golfer usually leaves his sand shots well short of the hole. So the next time you play in your usual weekend fourball, make a few friendly bets. Anyone who leaves his sand shots short has to pay 50 cents, or whatever, towards the drinks at the 19th hole. I promise you it won't be long before you're getting up and down in two with the best of us.

The Low, Spinning Shot

RIGHT: *Deloft your sand wedge by opening it just a little and by placing your hands in front of the ball.* CENTER RIGHT: *Cock your wrists early on the backswing.* BELOW RIGHT: *Strike close to the ball, about half an inch behind.* FAR RIGHT: *The ball will fly low and bite.*

IN DIFFICULT LIES

So far, so good. You're gaining confidence from the sand. You have a basic understanding of the technique involved to get out every time from a greenside bunker, to fly the ball high and short, or low and long, with bite or run. You've practiced a bit and your scoring has improved as you are approaching your sand shots positively.

But all that was from a good clean lie on firm sand. So what about problem lies? What if your ball is clinging to a slope or tucked under the lip of a bunker? Or worse still, if it's well and truly plugged? Well, you do have to make adjustments in all of those cases, but although important, they are only small variations in the basic method you have applied.

The Uphill Lie

Faced with an uphill lie on the sand, the first thing you must appreciate is that you have to swing along the line of the slope as closely as you can. You have to dig your feet well in, particularly your left foot, because if you sink in while you're swinging, you'll hit behind the ball and leave it in the bunker. To set yourself up level with the slope, you will then have to put more of your weight back on your right side, keeping your left shoulder up, and this will make swinging up through the sand very much easier.

You need to address the ball back as close to the center of your stance as possible, with your hands just a hair ahead of it, as you don't want to dig too deep into the sand before reaching the ball. If you straighten that leg as you swing, the slope will make you topple back to your right and the ball is likely to shoot straight up in the air.

Your stance should be open and your club face open as well, but you should also realize that a ball naturally flies much higher from an uphill lie with a lot of backspin, which will make it stop quickly. This is why most golfers leave their balls well short of the flag when playing from an upslope. So you must compensate for this in your aim and swing.

First, you could aim at an imaginary target area, or an imaginary flag, some two to three yards beyond the actual one. Second, you would have to swing with more force in your follow through, which will be restricted by the slope and can cause you to quit on the shot, virtually stopping just after impact. So you take a firmer grip on your club to allow for some

The Low, Running Shot

RIGHT: *For a low running shot, play the ball off the center of the stance.* BELOW RIGHT: *Keep your left wrist bent to the inside and don't break it on the follow through.* BOTTOM RIGHT: *Concentrate your weight on your left and keep your hands ahead of the ball. But use your pitching wedge, as its lesser loft gives the run.* CENTER RIGHT: *Stand close to the ball and aim to hit into the sand about half an inch behind the ball.* FAR RIGHT: *Remember to keep your left wrist firm through impact.*

jarring in your hands and hit harder, leading through the ball with your hands as much as possible.

After you've practiced this shot a few times, still entering the sand one and a half inches behind the ball, then try another way of making sure you get up to your target area. Using your usual force of swing for a ten-yard bunker shot, aim to strike the sand only one inch behind the ball and make sure that you follow through the shot completely. You will find that you have more control taking less sand and swinging smoothly, although you probably won't get past the hole too many times even then.

Under the Bunker Lip

When you find your ball under the front lip of a greenside bunker, the same set-up fundamentals apply as with the uphill lie. In this case you will need height to get over the lip, so you open your club face as much as possible. Then, instead of setting your hands slightly ahead of the ball at address, you set your hands level with, or slightly behind, it. This lets your right hand work under the left more, giving greater height on the shot.

But again you must remember that the most common error is in hitting fat or taking too much sand, so that the ball may not even clear the lip. You must make sure that your weight is well back on your right side to help you in hitting up along the line of the slope.

One of the best uphill bunker shots I have played was a crucial one at the 1974 JAL Open in Japan. On the 18th hole of the last round, I needed a par five to win the tournament. But, leaving myself a soft sand wedge from the fairway to the flag, I hit a horrible shot right into the face of a greenside bunker. Now four other players, including Peter Thomson, were tied for the lead and watching from the clubhouse at that moment.

On seeing my ball plummet into the bunker, they all started putting their shoes on, getting ready for a play off. But I got into the bunker, ground my feet well in, flexed my left leg, set my weight to the right, opened the club face and hit down firmly through the sand. The ball popped out and came down stone dead for a "gimme putt".

The Downhill Lie

It's difficult to know whether the uphill or the downhill lie in a bunker causes the most problems for the handicap golfer. On balance, it's probably the downhill lie, because many fear, from previous experience, that they will thin the ball into the face in front of them. However, worry not: the right technique will soon have you playing difficult downhill lies calmly and surely.

Downhill, you must also make the arc of your swing match the contour of the slope as much as possible. In other words, you stand with your shoulders and hips as level with the gradient as you can. So you set your weight on your left side and to help hold this position you kick your right knee in toward your left one. You also try consciously to keep your right shoulder up.

Because of the downhill slope, the ball comes out on a lower trajectory, so you have to hold your club face and stance well open. You address the ball opposite your right foot to make the plane of your swing as steep as possible. This is necessary to ensure you clear the lip of the bunker both going back and coming down and it helps you hit steeply down into the sand behind the ball. If you don't, you will almost certainly thin the ball farther into the bunker. Finally, you aim to enter the sand about three inches behind the ball and keep swinging, following the downhill slope of the bunker.

Clearly you have to pick the club up very quickly, with a very early wrist cock, and when you strike the match be conscious of swinging down at the same angle through the sand, making your hands lead down and through. The ball should come out relatively low and you should allow for plenty of run when it lands.

Now we all need some luck from time to time and one of my luckiest shots was from a downhill lie at the 12th hole of the 1965 Masters, the year Arnold Palmer and I finished joint second to Jack Nicklaus. The short 12th lies over the creek and, playing with Bob Murphy, I hit my tee shot over the green into the bunker behind the pin.

The green was as hard as a rock and very fast. The flag was on its right-hand corner, about eight feet short of the water. To make matters worse, when I got to the bunker I found that I had buried my ball under the back lip. I could only see the ball from the bottom of the bunker and when I addressed it, the lip screened the ball from sight.

I almost thought about declaring the ball unplayable, but I decided in the end to chop down on it, try and land it just over the greenside lip, and hope for the best with the run. At worst, I might just have duffed it down into the bottom of the bunker and there I would find a decent lie. So I hit

68

The Uphill Lie

FAR LEFT: *Dig your feet well in, with your weight back on your right side and your left shoulder up. Take a firm grip down on your club. Your stance and club face should be open.* LEFT: *At the top of the backswing, your club should not pass parallel of the slope.* BELOW FAR LEFT: *Swing with force in your follow through, hit hard and lead through the ball with your hands as much as possible.* BELOW LEFT: *Keep the left leg well flexed through the swing. The ball will fly high, with plenty of backspin.*

Under the Bunker Lip

RIGHT: *With a horrid, plugged lie at the front edge of the bunker, address the ball with an open stance. Play the ball off the right foot and hold the club face wide open.* FAR RIGHT: *Make sure that your weight is well back on your right side.* OVERLEAF AND FOLLOWING PAGE: *Hit down firmly into the sand and forget the follow through.*

The Downhill Lie from the Bunker Lip

RIGHT: *Buried under the back bunker lip - as I found my ball at Augusta in 1965 - you need to keep your shoulders level with the slope.* CENTER RIGHT: *Keep the club face squared to the target.* ABOVE FAR RIGHT: *Chop down on the ball.* FAR RIGHT: *Swing through the ball.* BELOW FAR RIGHT: *The ball will come out low, with run but you'll still need some luck to get near the hole.*

The Downhill Lie

PRECEDING PAGES, PAGES 76-77: *From a clean, downhill lie, open your stance, keep your weight left and "kick" your right knee in to hold steady as you swing. Open your club face and play the ball opposite your right foot, with an early wrist cock.* PAGES 78-81: *Swing down and through along the line of the downslope.*

down firmly into the sand and the ball shot out, landed just on the green, ran on, hit the flag and dropped into the hole for a two.

Now that was a lucky shot, but experience definitely played a hand. Had I tried to hit the flag, I would almost certainly have ended up in the water and at best would have made a double bogey. As it was, knowing the right techniques and experience in using them paid off.

The Ball above the Feet

When the ball is lying on sand above your feet when you build your stance, you cannot use your normal grip or alignment. Because you are standing below your ball, you will swing flatter and the ball will tend to pull left of your target or even hook a little.

So your first adjustment must be to grip the club shorter, go down the grip by at least three inches, if necessary all the way down to the bottom of the grip. This will ensure that the club doesn't dig too deeply into the sand, as well as keep your swing plane a little more upright.

The ball will still tend to go left however, so your second adjustment must be to align yourself well to the right of your target, anything from two to five feet depending on the severity of the slope. But you also have to make sure that you don't close the club face at impact, which would shove the ball even farther left.

The best way to avoid this is to weaken your right hand grip. Keeping the club face well open, with your hands in front of the ball, just move your right hand over to the left on the grip, so that the "V" formed by its thumb and index finger point to the left of your chin.

Everything else about your stance and swing is the same as with a normal bunker shot. Just remember, keep the overall action slow and smooth, strike the match firmly and follow through fully. Every good bunker player makes sure he follows through.

The Ball below the Feet

When the ball's below your feet, many opposite adjustments are needed. You are often reaching well below your feet and wishing your sand wedge was several inches longer than normal, so you have to hold it as long as possible, at the very end of the grip. To reach the ball more easily, and

82

above all to avoid the real danger of topping it, you also have to stand as close to it as you can.

You must also really "sit down" on the shot, flexing your knees as much as you can. If you are able to stand in the sand, rather than teeter on the grass bordering the bunker, you must also tread the sand down until you have a solid base and a firm footing.

Allow for the ball to slice or be pushed a little, so be sure to aim well left of your target area. But the really important adjustment about your set-up is to position the ball opposite your right foot, for if you play it off the left, that kills the shot.

You also have to swing a little harder, although you must keep a slow, smooth swing in mind and lead your hands down and through as much as possible. Throughout the swing, it's important that you keep your address position steady, with your head and body at the same level, knees always well flexed. That's a key in playing a tricky shot like this: it stops you from catching the ball too cleanly. The shot needs more smoothness than force.

The Plugged Lie

The bunker shot that is probably the most dreaded by golfers is the one from a plugged, or from a semi-buried, lie. They believe it needs considerable force to explode the ball out onto the green and in hitting so hard, they lose any control. In fact, it's not a question of hitting hard at all, not if you use the correct techniques, and the club face is going to do most of the work for you.

Just remember three things for all buried lies: you need a steep angle of attack, you need to square, not close, the club face and you must allow for run on the ball as there is no possible way to get backspin from a ball nestling in the sand. To put the amount of run into perspective, a ball that is splashed out from a clean lie runs some three to four feet. From a semi-buried lie, like a shallow footprint or a rake mark, it will run five times farther, some fifteen feet. But from a buried lie you would be lucky to get it to stop within thirty feet, ten times as far. So plan your shots accordingly.

To play the explosion shot, as it's often called, you set up with a slightly open stance, with your weight on your left foot. You should address the ball back in your stance toward the right foot, which automatically sets your hands ahead of it. This helps to create a very upright swing plane and

The Ball above the Feet

You will swing flatter and tend to pull the ball left. ABOVE FAR LEFT: Make sure you hold your club well down the grip. ABOVE CENTER LEFT: Align yourself well right of target. ABOVE LEFT: Take the club away in a straight line. ABOVE: Weaken your right hand grip to hold the club face open through the shot. FAR LEFT: Your set-up will compensate for the flatter swing plane and the right-to-left trajectory of the ball. LEFT: Follow through fully.

The Ball above the Feet Uphill

PRECEDING PAGES, PAGES 88 AND 89: *Get your left foot well up the slope and keep your weight well right to prevent hitting the ball fat and taking too much sand. Grip well down the shaft, stand slightly open.* PAGES 90 AND 91: *Hit firmly up the slope through the sand.*

The Ball below the Feet

OPPOSITE, RIGHT: *Hold your sand wedge at the top of the grip to reach the ball when it is below your feet.* ABOVE FAR RIGHT: *Settle down into the shot, flexing your knees as much as possible. Aim well left of target to allow for a slice. Play the ball off your right foot.* FAR RIGHT: *Your swing plane will have to be steep.* BELOW FAR RIGHT: *Swing a little harder, leading your hands down and through.*

a steep angle of attack down into the sand, which is essential in helping you get under the depression in which the ball sits.

The other really important adjustment to make is to negate the bounce on your sand wedge, the part of the club that protrudes below the leading edge. You don't need an open club face, because the sole of the club would then bounce off the sand into the back of the ball and bury it deeper into the greenside face, or sand will fly well over the green. So you must hold the club face square to your target, not closed as some people might try to tell you.

With our slow swing tempo you then take the club up steeply, making at least a three-quarter length backswing, to make sure you generate sufficient clubhead speed. Then you chop down firmly into the sand, about two inches behind the ball. The leading edge of your squared club face will cut through the sand like a knife, but don't even think about a follow through. You are hitting almost straight down into the sand and its resistance will stop your club face abruptly.

You do need to generate a degree of clubhead speed to force the ball out of a badly buried lie and you certainly must feel you are accelerating through the shot, striking the match firmly. But you must not smash your club into the sand. Just trust the squared club face to pop the ball out onto the front of the green from where it will run quickly toward the hole.

The lesson of "square the club face to pop the ball out" from a buried lie was clearly demonstrated at the 72nd hole of the Masters in 1961. All the drama of this great championship was packed into the 13th and 18th holes of the last round. At the 455-yard 13th, I had a three-shot lead over Arnold Palmer but hooked my 2-iron approach into the water in front of the green. Picking out under penalty, I pitched to the back of the green and then proceeded to three-putt for a seven. In one hole, my lead was wiped out and when I dropped another shot on the 15th I felt the championship had gone.

However, I then managed to scramble a couple of pars. At No. 18 though, I really had to hold my ragged nerves together. After a loose drive, I flopped my 4-iron approach into the bunker to the right of the green. I was pin high, but the flag was down a slippery slope at the bottom of the green, a very difficult shot under any circumstances. But I then played one of my most memorable bunker shots, splashing the ball out to within six feet of the hole and I sank the putt. This was one of the most harrowing I have ever had to make.

above all to avoid the real danger of topping it, you also have to stand as close to it as you can.

You must also really "sit down" on the shot, flexing your knees as much as you can. If you are able to stand in the sand, rather than teeter on the grass bordering the bunker, you must also tread the sand down until you have a solid base and a firm footing.

Allow for the ball to slice or be pushed a little, so be sure to aim well left of your target area. But the really important adjustment about your set-up is to position the ball opposite your right foot, for if you play it off the left, that kills the shot.

You also have to swing a little harder, although you must keep a slow, smooth swing in mind and lead your hands down and through as much as possible. Throughout the swing, it's important that you keep your address position steady, with your head and body at the same level, knees always well flexed. That's a key in playing a tricky shot like this: it stops you from catching the ball too cleanly. The shot needs more smoothness than force.

The Plugged Lie

The bunker shot that is probably the most dreaded by golfers is the one from a plugged, or from a semi-buried, lie. They believe it needs considerable force to explode the ball out onto the green and in hitting so hard, they lose any control. In fact, it's not a question of hitting hard at all, not if you use the correct techniques, and the club face is going to do most of the work for you.

Just remember three things for all buried lies: you need a steep angle of attack, you need to square, not close, the club face and you must allow for run on the ball as there is no possible way to get backspin from a ball nestling in the sand. To put the amount of run into perspective, a ball that is splashed out from a clean lie runs some three to four feet. From a semi-buried lie, like a shallow footprint or a rake mark, it will run five times farther, some fifteen feet. But from a buried lie you would be lucky to get it to stop within thirty feet, ten times as far. So plan your shots accordingly.

To play the explosion shot, as it's often called, you set up with a slightly open stance, with your weight on your left foot. You should address the ball back in your stance toward the right foot, which automatically sets your hands ahead of it. This helps to create a very upright swing plane and

PRECEDING PAGES,
PAGES 76-77: *From a
clean, downhill lie, open
your stance, keep your
weight left and "kick"
your right knee in to hold
steady as you swing.
Open your club face and
play the ball opposite
your right foot, with an
early wrist cock. PAGES
78-81: Swing down and
through along the line of
the downslope.*

down firmly into the sand and the ball shot out, landed just on the green, ran on, hit the flag and dropped into the hole for a two.

Now that was a lucky shot, but experience definitely played a hand. Had I tried to hit the flag, I would almost certainly have ended up in the water and at best would have made a double bogey. As it was, knowing the right techniques and experience in using them paid off.

The Ball above the Feet

When the ball is lying on sand above your feet when you build your stance, you cannot use your normal grip or alignment. Because you are standing below your ball, you will swing flatter and the ball will tend to pull left of your target or even hook a little.

So your first adjustment must be to grip the club shorter, go down the grip by at least three inches, if necessary all the way down to the bottom of the grip. This will ensure that the club doesn't dig too deeply into the sand, as well as keep your swing plane a little more upright.

The ball will still tend to go left however, so your second adjustment must be to align yourself well to the right of your target, anything from two to five feet depending on the severity of the slope. But you also have to make sure that you don't close the club face at impact, which would shove the ball even farther left.

The best way to avoid this is to weaken your right hand grip. Keeping the club face well open, with your hands in front of the ball, just move your right hand over to the left on the grip, so that the "V" formed by its thumb and index finger point to the left of your chin.

Everything else about your stance and swing is the same as with a normal bunker shot. Just remember, keep the overall action slow and smooth, strike the match firmly and follow through fully. Every good bunker player makes sure he follows through.

The Ball below the Feet

When the ball's below your feet, many opposite adjustments are needed. You are often reaching well below your feet and wishing your sand wedge was several inches longer than normal, so you have to hold it as long as possible, at the very end of the grip. To reach the ball more easily, and

The Ball above the Feet

You will swing flatter and tend to pull the ball left. ABOVE FAR LEFT: Make sure you hold your club well down the grip. ABOVE CENTER LEFT: Align yourself well right of target. ABOVE LEFT: Take the club away in a straight line. ABOVE: Weaken your right hand grip to hold the club face open through the shot. FAR LEFT: Your set-up will compensate for the flatter swing plane and the right-to-left trajectory of the ball. LEFT: Follow through fully.

The Ball Severely above the Feet

FAR LEFT: *When the ball lies well above your feet, stand tall.* BELOW FAR LEFT: *Hold your wedge at the very bottom of the grip to keep your swing plane a little more upright.* BOTTOM FAR LEFT: *Align yourself well to the right of your target.* CENTER LEFT: *Aim up to five feet right of your target area, keep the club face open and swing slow.* LEFT: *Follow through fully.*

PRECEDING PAGES,
PAGES 88 AND 89: *Get
your left foot well up the
slope and keep your
weight well right to
prevent hitting the ball
fat and taking too much
sand. Grip well down the
shaft, stand slightly open.*
PAGES 90 AND 91: *Hit
firmly up the slope
through the sand.*

The Ball below the
Feet

OPPOSITE, RIGHT:
*Hold your sand wedge at
the top of the grip to
reach the ball when it is
below your feet.* ABOVE
FAR RIGHT: *Settle down
into the shot, flexing your
knees as much as
possible. Aim well left of
target to allow for a slice.
Play the ball off your
right foot.* FAR RIGHT:
*Your swing plane will
have to be steep.* BELOW
FAR RIGHT: *Swing a
little harder, leading your
hands down and through.*

a steep angle of attack down into the sand, which is essential in helping you get under the depression in which the ball sits.

The other really important adjustment to make is to negate the bounce on your sand wedge, the part of the club that protrudes below the leading edge. You don't need an open club face, because the sole of the club would then bounce off the sand into the back of the ball and bury it deeper into the greenside face, or sand will fly well over the green. So you must hold the club face square to your target, not closed as some people might try to tell you.

With our slow swing tempo you then take the club up steeply, making at least a three-quarter length backswing, to make sure you generate sufficient clubhead speed. Then you chop down firmly into the sand, about two inches behind the ball. The leading edge of your squared club face will cut through the sand like a knife, but don't even think about a follow through. You are hitting almost straight down into the sand and its resistance will stop your club face abruptly.

You do need to generate a degree of clubhead speed to force the ball out of a badly buried lie and you certainly must feel you are accelerating through the shot, striking the match firmly. But you must not smash your club into the sand. Just trust the squared club face to pop the ball out onto the front of the green from where it will run quickly toward the hole.

The lesson of "square the club face to pop the ball out" from a buried lie was clearly demonstrated at the 72nd hole of the Masters in 1961. All the drama of this great championship was packed into the 13th and 18th holes of the last round. At the 455-yard 13th, I had a three-shot lead over Arnold Palmer but hooked my 2-iron approach into the water in front of the green. Picking out under penalty, I pitched to the back of the green and then proceeded to three-putt for a seven. In one hole, my lead was wiped out and when I dropped another shot on the 15th I felt the championship had gone.

However, I then managed to scramble a couple of pars. At No. 18 though, I really had to hold my ragged nerves together. After a loose drive, I flopped my 4-iron approach into the bunker to the right of the green. I was pin high, but the flag was down a slippery slope at the bottom of the green, a very difficult shot under any circumstances. But I then played one of my most memorable bunker shots, splashing the ball out to within six feet of the hole and I sank the putt. This was one of the most harrowing I have ever had to make.

The Ball below the Feet on the Knees

RIGHT: *Sometimes you may have an impossible lie, with the ball so far below your feet that you have to kneel and play. At least from this position, you can't sway very much and your feet won't slip.* OVERLEAF: *Play the ball off your right knee, aim left and swing hard.*

The Plugged Lie

OPPOSITE, RIGHT: *A foot print or a rake mark or simply very fluffy sand require a slightly different approach.* CENTER RIGHT: *When the ball is plugged, play it off your right foot, with a slightly open stance, weight left. Keep the club face square.* ABOVE FAR RIGHT: *Take the club up steeply with a three-quarter swing.* RIGHT: *Chop down firmly into the sand, two inches behind the ball.* FAR RIGHT: *There is no follow through. As you hit straight into the sand, its resistance will stop the clubhead abruptly. The squared club face will pop the ball out.*

By now, out on the 15th, Arnold had a one-shot lead and he later walked onto the 18th tee needing a par four to win. He hit a great drive, but then faded his 7-iron approach into the same right-hand bunker I had been in and the ball finished up in a buried lie.

At this time I was watching the TV coverage in the clubhouse with Bobby Jones and I could scarcely believe my eyes when I saw Arnold address his ball in the bunker. He was setting up to play the buried lie with a wide open club face. Bobby Jones said: "He should square the face and pop it out." But Arnold hit down into the sand with the club wide open and skulled the ball right over the green and down a slope. He did chip it back to five yards, but he then missed the putt and I won the Masters.

In retrospect, while I was sad for Arnold, losing because of such an unaccountable mental lapse, I also realized the significance of my own bunker shot on the 18th. I had applied the right fundamentals and I never gave up on the shot. Just remember, whenever you're faced with a buried lie, square the club face.

The Shot from Wet Sand

If you have winced at finding your ball in a greenside bunker in a plugged lie, you would certainly groan to find the ball lying in wet sand, or on a compacted surface, or worse still, sitting slightly down in soft, fluffy sand. Any difficult sand surface from the norm instantly evokes ideas of the club skidding off or digging in futilely, but almost all the problems only exist in the mind. The right technique will banish them forever.

In wet sand you have to play the shot you normally would in good conditions, only you have to swing easier, because the club is going to skid off the sand. So you swing softer. In other words, if you're faced with a ten-yard shot, you play it as though it was only seven yards. With the skid, the ball will come out much faster, so swing easier.

The Shot from Hard Sand

On a hard surface, where there is little depth to the sand in the bunker, or if it's too compacted or frozen, it's no use to attempt your standard splash shot. If you do, the sole of your sand wedge is going to hit the hard ground and bounce on it, shooting the ball off anywhere, with little height.

But you need to open the club face and you must have a steep angle of attack on the sand, still some one and a half inches behind the ball. You

***The Plugged Ball
above the Feet
Uphill***

PRECEDING PAGES,
PAGE 100: *With the ball
plugged above your feet,
square the club face and
keep your weight right in
a slightly open stance.*
PAGE 101: *"Strike the
match" firmly.* PAGE
102: *The ball will jump
up promptly....* PAGE
103: *..and run quickly
toward the hole.*

play it off the center of your stance and again you swing very easily. The ball will shoot out fast, so if you're faced with a ten-yard shot to your target, play it as though it was only five yards away.

Escape from Fluffy Sand

You also need a steep swing in soft, or fluffy, sand only in this case you get virtually no follow through. When bunkers are newly filled with sand, or the sand hasn't had a chance to pack down well, a ball will often settle down in its own pitch mark and you then have to play it a little like an explosion shot.

You need to square the club face and set up with the ball in the center of your stance, which should be very open. Keep your weight on your left foot and swing down firmly, but not too hard into the sand. The feel is like the little chop you make when you block a table tennis ball with backspin. If you hit too hard, you'll mess it up.

You should aim to enter the sand as close to the ball as possible, maybe half an inch behind it, cutting down deeply to finish with the clubhead in the sand just past the ball's original position. As you've gone in steeply, the ball will jump out steeply too. It will have little backspin, but it will fly high, drop softly on the green and won't have much run. As with the other shots from difficult lies, it's a very useful one to have in your golf bag.

IN THE FAIRWAY BUNKER

"Oh, no. Don't go in there!" is a wail frequently heard on the tee. It happens when a golfer watches his drive falling inexorably on the line of a distant fairway bunker. The long walk toward it is filled with thoughts of "is the ball plugged?" or "maybe it's under the front lip?". All is very stressful, for this is one of the most difficult situations to be in and at certain times it can blow a match, be it a friendly one, or a championship, never mind a major.

It happened to me on the 18th hole of the 1959 British Open. It was played at Muirfield, an outstanding course, criss-crossed by stone dikes, stretching 6,800 yards along the sandhills of the Firth of Forth. Very Scottish, it has hundreds of bunkers and I had the critical ones on each hole carefully filed, with a clear plan on how best to avoid them in varying weather, never mind the prevailing hard westerlies. On the last hole of the last round, for which I was six under par, I felt sure I only needed a par four to win. It was simple: 427 yards, bunker on the right in driving range, three other fairway bunkers on the left, narrow fairway, banked green.

Confidently, I hit a reasonable drive down the left … but it didn't fade as much as I told it to and caught a left-hand bunker, going in about a foot. Then I played a really poor shot, one of the worst fairway bunker shots I had ever played, knocking the ball out with a 6-iron some hundred yards up the fairway. Another six to the edge of the green and three putts left me utterly disconsolate. All I had needed was a straightforward four. I had made six and my entire world seemed to disintegrate.

However, the third round leaders still had a good nine holes to play in stormy weather. I had to wait for an agonizing two hours before they approached the final green, and by then everything had changed. There, the tough Belgian Flory van Donck missed a 40-foot putt to tie me. I was the Open Champion! But I never forgot that for two long hours I believed I had thrown the championship away, all because of that dreadful fairway bunker shot.

Since then I have learned to play all types of shots from fairway bunkers fairly well. So can you, given a grounding in the right techniques and a little practice. You need never be apprehensive again, if you remember that the operative word is fairway. For if your lie is good, with almost every shot off fairway sand, the ball should be struck as if it were lying on

OVERLEAF, TOP LEFT: *Playing with a long iron from a fairway bunker you set up square to slightly open, keeping your weight on your left and the ball centered. Keep your head still and aim at the top half of the ball.* TOP RIGHT: *Don't rush on your downswing. Keep your head still. You must hit the ball 100 per cent clean, with the feeling you are thinning it.* BELOW LEFT: *The ball will fly a little lower than it normally would.* BELOW RIGHT: *Follow through fully.*

clipped grass. The ball should be caught cleanly and the divot of sand taken after impact.

The Clean, Long Iron Shot

Before getting down to the specifics of the stroke, there are a few considerations to take into account. As with a greenside bunker shot, you have to read the sand carefully and consider the target area you want to aim at. Weather conditions could affect this, as could the club you might have to use, so club selection is very important.

First you have to look at your lie. If the ball is sitting down in a depression, you don't have an option: you will have to take your sand wedge and play it like a long sand shot, making sure you get out and down the fairway as far as possible. But if your ball is sitting up on firm sand, you must look at how far it is lying from the front lip of the bunker and the height of this lip. The ball will fly lower than with a normal shot, so you must select a club that will allow it to clear the lip with a good margin of safety. If you have any doubt that a 5-iron will give enough height, say, take a six to be sure.

You must then consider how far you have to hit the ball and if the club you might have to take will allow you to reach your target area on the green. The weather conditions, especially if it is very windy, might well affect your club selection. Wind can wreck swings, as golfers tend to swing faster and faster when it blows up. Thrashing at the ball is never good at the best of times, but it is very bad for fairway bunker shots in particular. In all cases remember: when it's breezy, swing easy.

Playing into a blustery headwind, you must take plenty of club to reach your target area. The yardage difference between clubs, normally about ten, is cut by 30 per cent into a strong wind, so overclubbing should not be a problem. Crosswinds, however, must be considered. If it's blowing right to left, you must allow for this by at least aiming right and letting the wind bring the ball back in. Better still, you should aim to hold the ball up against the wind by fading it, with its spin going in the opposite direction. You would obviously aim left, or play a slight draw, with right to left spin, if the wind was coming from the opposite direction, i.e. left to right.

So having decided, say, that you could reach the center of the green, 150 yards away and that your 5-iron is the club to clear the bunker's front lip and carry any greenside bunkers safely, as there is only a very slight breeze from your right, let's get down to the specifics of the stroke. First you have to set up with a slightly wider stance than usual, with your feet well dug in, especially the inside of the right foot to fix the entire right side firmly throughout the stroke. This helps you to minimize body movement, weight shift and leg action during the swing, for you've got to stay very steady over the ball.

Your feet and shoulders should be square to slightly open, as should your club face. With a little more weight on your left foot than normal, you should position the ball in the center of your stance, with your hands slightly forward of the clubhead. But don't overdo any of these factors in the address. You should feel comfortable and confident when you stand over the ball.

You don't have to cock your wrists too quickly on the takeaway and you must not overswing. You move mainly your arms and upper body and make a three-quarter swing. But you must keep your head still over the ball, which prevents you from swaying. If you sway at all in the sand, you're gone. To help you keep your head still you should focus your eyes on the front of the ball, which also ensures that you hit it as cleanly as possible and not even touch the sand first.

You must not rush the downswing, despite any apprehension you might feel. You simply swing your arms down and through, aiming to catch the ball 100 per cent clean and then take a small divot of sand, as you would on a normal fairway shot. To make certain that you don't hit the ball fat, you should try and have the feeling that you're hitting it thinly, in fact almost topping it. You almost certainly won't thin it, but, well-struck, its flight will be a little lower than that of a normal shot.

Should you want to play a similar shot with a higher trajectory however, all you have to do is position the ball a little farther forward, playing it off your left heel, with your hands level with it. You may not be able to focus your eyes on the front of the ball, but you will still have to hit it cleanly. So aim to hit the top half to avoid hitting fat and it should head unwaveringly toward the green.

The Long Shot for High Handicappers

Working the ball out of the sand can really be very satisfying, but if you are a high handicapper you might feel you need just one super safe shot to ensure you always get out with a bit of distance. To play this, providing you have no problems in clearing the front lip of the bunker, select your 5-iron

The Long, High Shot

OVERLEAF, PAGE 110, TOP LEFT: *Stand slightly open and play the ball off your left heel for a long, high shot from fairway sand. Your hands should be level with the ball.* TOP RIGHT: *You'll need a wider stance to minimize body movement.* PAGE 111, TOP LEFT: *Make a three-quarter swing.* PAGE 110, BELOW LEFT: *Catch the ball cleanly.* BELOW RIGHT: *Take a divot of sand after impact.* PAGE 111, BELOW RIGHT: *Follow through fully.*

and set up with your feet, shoulders and club face square, and your weight favoring your left foot.

You should play the ball way back in your stance, positioning it just a little ahead of your right heel, while keeping your hands in their normal address position off the inside of your left leg. This places your hands well ahead of the ball, which means effectively that you are hooding the club face, taking loft off it, maybe as much as two clubs' worth. So if your shot calls for the distance of a 5-iron, hood a seven, while the 5-iron you have chosen will give you the distance of a three.

Keep your eyes fixed on the sand about one inch in front of the ball and, as before, keep your head still to avoid any sway. Swing slow and with this set-up you'll find it virtually impossible to hit the sand before the ball. You'll catch the ball 100 per cent clean and send it a long way down toward the green. It may not look like a very elegant shot, but it's a safe one if you need distance from fairway sand.

The Fairway Wood Shot

If you need a lot more distance, from a fairway bunker on a long par five say, then you will have to play a wood. Most club golfers should find it easier to play a fairway wood under most conditions than a long iron. With a good lie on the fairway, that's to say with a good amount of grass between ball and ground, there's no problem. It doesn't matter if the bottom of the clubhead hits the bottom of the ball exactly flush or swings through a small distance beneath it. If the lie is tight though, with the ball almost resting on the bare ground, the fairway wood is even more tolerant. Where the leading edge of a long iron will cut into the ground, the sole of a 5-wood will generally slide along the surface, giving a good result with a less than perfect contact. The same principle applies if you're playing off sand, providing you apply the right technique.

In this case, using your 5-wood to be sure of getting out of a fairway bunker and gaining good distance, you set up with a shoulder-wide stance. Dig your feet well in, with your weight now slightly more on your right foot than if you were playing your 5-iron. Your feet and shoulders should be aligned to point left of the target, in an open position and you should open the club face quite wide, three-quarters of an inch or so, before taking your normal grip, choking down on the club a little to allow for your feet being lower in the sand.

You play the ball off your left heel and in this case aim to strike the sand about an inch to an inch and a half behind it. With any club, by opening the club face you lower the back of the sole so that it strikes the ground first. In other words, you can create some bounce, even on a flat-soled club, so that it skids through the sand. This is what happens when you play a wood from a fairway bunker in this manner. The open club face tilts the club so that the back of its sole hits the sand before its leading edge and the club skids through just like a sand wedge. You should get quite a fair distance with this technique, although you'll also get a high fade in all probability, if not a slice.

The Fade

The ability to fade or draw a ball can be very useful, particularly if you catch a fairway bunker at the corner of a dog-leg and have to work your ball out and around trees toward the green. To fade the ball gently left to right, so that it moves only a few feet away from a dead straight line through the air and then curves gently back, usually means a high-flying shot that lands on the green with plenty of backspin. The draw (not the hook!) coming in slightly from right to left, can be every bit as accurate and is a more powerful shot.

Few golfers, however, really understand just why they hit the ball in a way that invariably spins it either to the left or to the right. When, for example, they overdo the left to right movement of a fade and produce an inaccurate, wildly spinning slice that finishes well right of the target, they rarely think that their stance is too open, as is the club face at contact. Instead, they shuffle about and aim feet, hips and shoulders even more to the left, in an effort to keep their ball on the fairway. But this opens the stance even farther, producing an even more uncontrolled slice on their next shot.

They have never been taught how to interpret the pattern of shots they produce. So perhaps it is worthwhile to consider the theory and techniques of what makes a ball spin left to right, or right to left. This will teach you how you can create a controlled spin to greatly improve your shotmaking.

The first thing to realize is that everyone has a natural shape of shot. Most golfers, some 80 per cent, hit the ball left to right, mostly as a slice rather than a power fade. If that's the case, don't fight it! Just learn how to control it. A straight shot is the hardest to play. It's better to have a

The Long Shot for High Handicappers

ABOVE RIGHT: *For the high handicapper's sure shot, play the ball back in your stance, with the hands ahead of the ball. As you're hooding the club face, you'll need a more lofted club.* ABOVE CENTER RIGHT: *Make a complete backswing but don't pass parallel to the ground.* RIGHT: *On the downswing, keep your eyes fixed on the sand one inch ahead of the ball. Swing slow.* FAR RIGHT: *Hit the ball clean.*

consistent shape of shot, even if it always ends up heading right. That way, if there's trouble on the left, say, you can play toward it and let your fade or slice bring the ball back safely to the center of the fairway. This gives you more room to play with off the tee and you will be more accurate playing to the green. But you should know how to bend the flight of the ball the other way, as you will often need to do so during the course of a round.

So let's consider the fade, where the ball starts out left of the target line and then spins back to the right. Now the initial flight to the left can be due to a number of reasons. The golfer could simply be aiming left, finding it easier to see the target with shoulders open. Or else, the ball could be positioned too far forward in the stance. This means it is struck after the clubhead is swinging back inside the target line again, heading left. It could also be due to an incomplete pivot in the backswing, so that the club at the top points to the left of the target. As a result, the downswing follows this line and sends the ball astray.

For the ball to then spin to the right though, there is basically only one reason: an open club face at contact, pointing to the right of the line of the swing. This means that when the club face contacts the ball it applies a cutting action, coming across the line from the club face to the target. The swing need not be from out-to-in, but the ball is compressed toward its part furthest away from the golfer, which puts a right to left curve on the ball.

There are several potential reasons for this, particularly with club golfers. The club face may have been wrongly aimed open at address, if the golfer didn't line it up carefully, and so remained open through contact. A weak grip is another main cause. This is when the "V" between the thumb and index fingers of each hand point left of the chin, causing the right hand to be behind the club at impact, leaving the club face open.

Tension is often also to blame. If the golfer is clutching onto the club too tightly, so that his hands and arms are too rigid, he or she is unable to release through the ball. As a result, the left arm usually leads through the downswing, breaking outward rather than folding naturally, and so the club face does not square up at impact. Finally, and especially with handicap players, clubs that are either too stiff or too heavy can be to blame. They do not make it easy to swing freely and often leave the club face open, particularly that of the driver.

These then are the accidental reasons why a golfer slices a ball, and it follows that if you want to produce a controlled fade you must start the ball left and contact it with an open club face. You must therefore set up with

edge of the left hand, seems to be a more powerful action than they can get with an easy release. So they hold the club with the left hand very much on top and the right well under, but at impact their hands turn instinctively more to the left, the wrists roll over and the club face closes.

The wrists can also roll over for two other reasons. The body of a golfer with a very flat swing will sometimes get in the way of his arms on the downswing, forcing an early release and wrist roll. A dominant right side is the other cause, where the left hand and arm are quite simply overpowered by the right, so that the right hand turns over the left just before contact.

Once again, these are the often accidental reasons why a ball will draw or hook from right to left - and you need to apply the same principles if you want to produce a controlled draw. That is to say that you have to set up aimed slightly right of target to start your shot off in that direction and then contact the ball with a closing club face to produce the right to left spin. You should set up with the ball back in your stance from your left heel by two or three inches to ensure that you're hitting it very slightly from the inside. Amateurs could aim the club face square to the target, although I prefer to strengthen my grip just a little, which brings the draw quite naturally.

It's a more powerful shot than the fade, generally giving a player an extra ten to thirty yards in distance, which is why it would certainly suit the older, or less strong, golfer. It also suits many top tournament players, like Arnold Palmer, Seve Ballesteros and myself. The great South African champion Bobby Locke also favored it for all his shots. Although he played very successfully with a fade as an amateur, he decided he needed more power when he became a professional, if he wanted to be a winner. So he started to play the draw, setting up with a very closed stance - body pointing to the right by some 45 degrees - and his effective technique brought him four British Open championships.

The High Fade

So now, having practiced the fade and the draw, how do you play them from a fairway bunker with, say, 150 yards to go to the center of the green? Let's just review the technique for the sand shot. First, if the lie is good and the lip of the bunker not too high, you should select your 4- or 5-iron for either shot.

To play a controlled, high-flying fade, you set up with the ball off your left heel and your stance a little open, feet and shoulders pointing left of your

The High Fade

RIGHT: *Set the ball off your left heel with your stance a little open.* OPPOSITE, RIGHT: *Weaken your grip by moving your left hand half an inch to the left.* CENTER AND FAR RIGHT: *To set your swing on the right path, take your club away along the line of your feet.* BELOW RIGHT: *Avoid swaying and strike the ball clean.* BELOW FAR RIGHT: *You will take some sand after you hit the ball.*

PRECEDING PAGES, PAGES 118-119, TOP LEFT: *With the wood from fairway sand, keep your weight right, standing open. Open the club face by three quarters of an inch and choke down the grip a little.* TOP RIGHT: *Take the club away as you would on the fairway.* BELOW: *The backswing should be wide and complete.* PAGES 120-121: *Play the ball off your left heel, hitting it clean.*

the line of your feet, hips and shoulders pointing slightly left of your target line, with the ball positioned off your left heel. You are then advised to aim the club face square to the target, but I prefer to aim it left also, along the line of my feet and shoulders. I advocate that you should just weaken your left hand grip by turning it about half an inch to the left to produce the desired spin, as this grip holds the club face slightly open through impact. Then you just swing normally, making sure the club comes through along the line of your feet and you will naturally produce a controlled fade.

It's a very reliable shot, the "bread and butter" for many top pros, especially Lee Trevino. You have to practice it to perfect it and remember that the lofted clubs don't give you any significant spin, so don't try to fade the ball if you have to play an 8-iron or less. You will only finish up left of the target, as the backspin will override the sidespin. You should take a club more than usual when playing the fade, as the shape of the shot cuts the distance you will get by some ten yards.

The Draw

The controlled draw, where the ball starts out slightly to the right of the target line and then moves back in purposefully, is in many ways a mirror image to the fade, although some of the causes of the spin are different. Shots start to the right of target mainly because the swing is aimed right at set-up, often only with the shoulders. If the club face is square at contact, the ball simply flies straight right; if it's open, you get a push slice. The ball position at address is also critical. Handicap players who sometimes block their shots to the right tend to play the ball too far back towards their right foot, so the club face contacts it while it is still swinging from the inside.

Blocking also occurs when the left side doesn't turn in time with the arms on the downswing. With a correct downswing, the hips are opening as the arms and club swing down and through. Some golfers however don't transfer their weight correctly, so that the line of their hips faces to the right of the target line at impact, pushing the ball straight out to the right.

The position of the club face at impact is again critical when it comes to putting spin on the ball, curving it from right to left. For this pattern of spin, it must be slightly closed at impact, facing a little left of the line of feet, hips and shoulders. Sometimes this is caused by the golfer aiming the club wrongly at address. Most often however, it is due to a grip that is a little too strong. Some golfers, particularly those with weak hands or wrists, feel comfortable gripping the club with both hands turned more to the right than they should be. Swinging down and through, hitting with the

PRECEDING PAGES,
PAGES 126-127, LEFT:
*Place the ball toward the
center of your stance to
keep the ball low. Your
shoulders, hips and feet
should point a little to the
left of your target to
impart the sidespin on the
ball.* CENTER: *Aim the
club face left to the
target. Swing your club in
a controlled manner,
drawing it along the line
of your feet.* RIGHT:
*Make at least a three-
quarter swing.* PAGES
128-129, LEFT: *Don't
swing too fast or hard.*
CENTER: *The club face
should be slightly open
through impact for the
left-to-right trajectory.*
RIGHT: *Complete your
follow through.*

target line. You should weaken your normal grip just a fraction. In other words, move your left hand on the club about half an inch to the left. Your club face is square to the line of your feet and shoulders, but your weaker grip will produce the fade, bending the ball from left to right. Take the club away along the line of your feet to set your swing on the right path. Once again, you will have to avoid any sway or excessive body movement and strike the ball absolutely clean, taking sand after you have hit it.

Although you want the ball to soar, bear in mind that the lofted clubs from the 8-iron to the wedges don't impart enough sidespin for a fade or a draw. Therefore, take a longer club even for the high fade as both the left-to-right spin and the height of your shot will curtail your distance.

The Low Fade

The low fade is a challenging shot as the sidespin of a fade usually results in a high trajectory. So you are contending here with two opposing forces. You will succeed if you make the correct adjustments to your stance.

Initially, the address position for this resembles the one for the high fade with the line of your feet, hips and shoulders pointing a little left of your target line. However, instead of placing the ball opposite your left heel, this time the ball is positioned an inch or two toward the center of your stance to produce the low trajectory of the ball.

Again, aim the club face left to the target also, along the line of your feet and shoulders. Don't forget to weaken your left hand grip by turning it about half an inch to the left. This grip ensures that the club face will be slightly open through impact and thus produce the desired sidespin. Then you just swing in the same controlled manner, drawing the club along the line of your feet.

But don't swing too fast or hard on either shot. When you do smash down on the ball, not only do you risk striking the sand first, but you could well negate the effect of the left-to-right spin you would impart, hitting the ball straight left instead.

The High Draw

Here is another shot that demands a little effort. The sidespin of the draw drags the ball down while you are trying to get it up into the air. Again, the key lies in the set-up. Align your body and clubhead slightly right of target

The High Draw

RIGHT: *Align your body and clubhead a little right of the target in the direction you want to start. Play the ball off your left heel.* BELOW RIGHT: *Use a stronger grip for the draw by turning your right hand to the right.* BOTTOM RIGHT: *Concentrate your weight on the left foot but keep your head behind the ball through impact.* CENTER RIGHT: *Swing mainly your arms, with very little body movement. This will close the club face earlier at impact, giving the right-to-left spin.* FAR RIGHT: *Follow through freely.*

The Draw

LEFT: *For a draw, you will need a good lie. Set up with your feet, shoulders and club face aimed to the right of your target, with the ball near the center of your stance so that you swing slightly from the inside.* BELOW LEFT: *Strengthening your grip produces a natural draw.* ABOVE CENTER LEFT AND FAR LEFT: *Take the club away along the line of your feet. Swinging mainly with your arms will promote the draw. Don't forget to finish your follow through so that your ball carries the distance you need.*

in the direction you want your ball to start out on. For the high draw, you position the ball a couple of inches off your left heel. Strengthen your grip, turning your right hand to the right, as if you were revving up a motorcycle. Swinging mainly with your arms, with a restricted body movement, will promote a draw and your stronger grip will tend to close the club face a little earlier, producing the required right-to-left spin. Remember that the draw will produce a longer roll on the ground, giving a player an extra ten to thirty yards in distance. You, therefore, need to select your club accordingly.

The Low Draw

Use the same set-up as for the high draw with your body aligned to the right of your target, and strengthen your grip by turning your right hand to the right. This will ensure that the club face closes through impact if you take your club away along the line of your feet. For a low draw all you need to do is play the ball a little farther back in your stance, but once again remember to swing slow as too hard a hit will simply push the ball straight right.

Bear in mind that you can't finesse a draw as easily as you can a fade, so be prepared for the ball to run a lot farther than it might normally. Remember to take this into account when you select your club. Finally, if you need to exaggerate the swing of the ball through the air, to hook it wide around an obstacle, all you should do is square or slightly close the club face to your intended line of flight. This will give you a big hook and you should personally find out just how much diversion you can put on the flight of the ball through a little practice session.

The Punch Shot

Another very useful way of working the ball from fairway bunker to green is with the punch shot. This flies very low and holds its line well, so it's a great shot to play in blustery conditions, particularly into the wind. You can also play it from the sand if your lie isn't all that good. It can be effective in getting out of the rough as well.

To play it you set up square to your target line, with your club face square and some 70 per cent of your weight on your left foot. The ball is positioned in the center of your stance, so that your hands are well ahead of it. You need to grip your club very firmly to avoid too much wrist action, which could flick the ball high in the air.

The Low Draw

FAR LEFT: *For the low draw, align your body to the right of your target. Keep your weight on the left of your body.*
CENTER LEFT: *Play the ball back in your stance and swing slow to avoid pushing the ball straight right.* LEFT: *Allow for a lot of run.*

During the three-quarter backswing you should concentrate on keeping your head still and avoid any swaying, as with all shots from the sand. Your address position will ensure that the club is picked up quickly, and on the downswing you have to strike down on the head of the ball. Chop down on it, making sure that your right arm is straight at impact so that your club follows through close to the ground. The right hand barely crosses over the left on the shot. At the finish, both arms should point at the hole.

With this swing the ball comes out of the sand quail-high, keeping well below the wind. As a result, it will often go farther into the wind than a normal full shot. In the British Open at St. Andrews in 1995, I punched a number of 3-irons that barely went two feet off the ground. On the 15th, playing with Raymond Floyd, I needed a full 3-wood to reach the green, but I thought that if I really hit it, the ball would balloon in the strong headwind. So I punched a 3-iron, the ball shot away two feet off the ground and I got the same distance as a full 3-wood into the air.

Sandy Lyle did not play safe in the 1988 Masters at Augusta, but he hit a very effective and elegant shot from the fairway bunker on the 18th hole of his last round. Considering the pressure, it was one of the greatest bunker shots ever played. Every golfer can benefit from an appreciation of his determination and technique.

Lyle stood on the 18th tee knowing he needed a par four to tie Mark Calcavecchia or a birdie to win the Masters. The 420-yard par four hole had trees along the right and two fairway bunkers guarding the left, the outside of the dog-leg. It seemed essential to keep the ball in play, so Lyle chose to tee off with his 1-iron, which he hit with power and accuracy on most occasions.

He aimed to fade the ball gently into the center of the fairway, but instead drew it a fraction and the ball skipped into the nearer of the fairway bunkers on the left. Thoroughly despondent at that moment, Lyle told his caddie that he felt he had blown the championship, as he doubted he could get onto the green from there.

When he reached the bunker, however, it looked as though he might have a chance if he played positively. The ball was lying cleanly on the sand, although it was fairly close to the front lip and he had 142 yards to the front of the green, with the flag a farther eight yards on. Lyle calculated that the least lofted club he needed to clear the lip and give him the yardage was his 8-iron. He then selected his 7-iron as he aimed to play a fade, which rises quickly, flies higher and doesn't go as far.

Working his feet firmly into the sand, he took an open stance and, holding his club face slightly open, aimed to play the ball back toward his right foot. With more weight on his left side, he then made a slow, steep three-quarter backswing and swung down smoothly, striking the ball cleanly before taking very little sand. The ball flew like an arrow over the flag and spun to a halt on the top of a ridge that ran across the width of the putting surface. After a long moment it began to roll slowly back toward the hole, finally stopping some ten feet from it.

When Sandy Lyle holed that slippery downhill putt, he became the first British winner at Augusta, thanks largely to that telling bunker shot. He said afterward: "Luckily the ball was up the slope of the sand and I had a good lie. I knew that if I could get it past the flag it would roll back toward the hole. I timed the shot just right and it came out perfectly."

That sort of timing comes with a little practice. If you practice the right techniques for sand play, you too should be able to make birdies from fairway bunkers. But with the right game plan, you should always aim to avoid them if you can. This is exactly what Ian Woosnam did on that 18th hole at Augusta in the final round of the 1991 Masters.

He was in a better position than Sandy Lyle had been three years earlier, as he had a one-shot lead over the field and knew that a par was all he needed to win. But unlike Lyle, the Welshman had decided that he would not even flirt with the dangerous fairway bunkers on the dog-leg. A noted long hitter, he smashed his drive well to the left and beyond them. The ball landed in some light rough, in what used to be a practice area, giving him an easy approach shot to the green. Woosnam duly two-putted to win the hole and the Championship.

An intelligent game plan, which plots the best way to play each hole, clearly avoids all the dangerous fairway bunkers. But when it goes wrong and you find yourself in the sand, don't despair. Play positively, for you can still win the hole - and the match.

The Punch Shot

RIGHT: *Grip down on the club for more control.* CENTER RIGHT: *Set up square for the punch shot, with your weight well on your left.* BELOW RIGHT: *With the ball in the center of your stance, your hands should be ahead. Grip firmly to avoid too much wrist action.* FAR RIGHT: *Pick up the club quickly.* BELOW CENTER RIGHT AND BELOW FAR RIGHT: *On the downswing, chop down on the ball. Remember to keep your right arm straight at impact.*

Practice

PRACTICE WITH A PURPOSE

Very few weekend golfers have any concept of what is meant by practice. Some run out to a local driving range once a month or so, for what they call a practice session. Their idea is to hit a bucket of balls, invariably with their driver, as hard and as fast as they can. When they thin one ball along the ground, they quickly tee up another, only to top it as badly as the first. They seem to feel that if they hit enough balls quickly they will eradicate any faults and improve their swing. What they are doing however is meaningless, without any thought or purpose behind it and they are probably grooving in some basic faults in their swings that will take effort to correct. That is not practice.

Nor is the golf course the right place for practice. On many a weekend round when a golfer slices his first few shots, he starts to brood about it. "Did I sway?" he thinks, "Or did I hold on too hard with the left hand?" After the next slice, he reconsiders: "Maybe I pulled across it, or drove too quickly with my legs?" From then on he practices not swaying or pulling across, oblivious to the fact that he is actually playing a game. He doesn't concentrate on his next shot, nor the target area he should be aiming for. All he can think of is to practice his swing, so it is little wonder that he scores in the high nineties.

All of that should be left for the practice ground. There is a time for practice and that's the place. All professional golfers use it to practice all the time. They warm up on the range, before and after each tournament round, often honing one particular shot, like a high fade, that is the shot to play on many of the holes of the course. But they will also spend time chipping or practicing sand shots, even if this is a strength, and they will certainly hit putt after putt from all distances to the cup on the practice putting green.

Many professionals enjoy practice and for others it's a way of life. I remember that in 1958 when I finished second in the US Open, I played one round with Ben Hogan. In the locker room afterward, he said: "Well, that was very well played. Make sure you practice hard. I never stop practicing." Nor have I, from the time I started to play golf.

There's no fast way to become a better golfer overnight. I am totally convinced that practice is the only way to improve any part of your game, especially bunker play. In South Africa, before I started to compete in tournaments around the world, I'd spend several hours a day practicing, as I still do. I take a bag of old balls out, dump them in a bunker and set myself a goal, say, to hole five shots. Once I've achieved that, I'll work on another part of my game. Sometimes I'll hole five fairly quickly, whereas other times I'll be there quite a while and only hole one.

I'll never forget the time when I was practicing at home, where we always had a bunker and a putting green in the garden. Some friends were coming over for dinner that night, but I thought that I would give myself an hour before they arrived to hole five shots from the sand. I holed three fairly quickly, then a fourth. Then our guests came, but I just couldn't hole the fifth. When my wife came out to drag me in about forty minutes later, I told her to "start without me, if you have to, but I'm not coming in until I hole another shot." As you can see, I believe in setting yourself targets when you're practicing, targets that you have to achieve.

I know that the average golfer has very little time for golf, and when he does get away from home or work, he wants to enjoy playing the game. The last thing he fancies is to spend an hour or two in isolation on the practice ground. I'd feel the same in his shoes. But one thing is sure: however talented you are, if you really want to improve your game, you have to practice with a purpose. There is no gain without pain and the practice ground is the arena.

The Practice in the Sand

From the start, you should realize that there are at least two ways of planning your practice sessions. The first is to zero in on those parts of your game that really need work and to concentrate only on those shots as your goals. The second is to practice a range of the most difficult shots, from the most awkward lies to the easiest, so that you become familiar with them and develop confidence. Neither way excludes the other. Over a period of time, you should practice in both ways if you really want to improve your game.

To find out which parts of your game you should work on, you'll need some data. Keep a record of the strokes you play over your next three or four rounds if you have not done so already. When you come to analyze your shots, you may get quite a surprise. For example, many players seem to think they need to improve their driving, but you might find that you've hit most of the fairways off the tee. You've squandered shots instead by three-putting four or five greens, fluffing a few short pitches and leaving your ball in three greenside and two fairway bunkers. You will then have to concentrate on your short game, devoting at least one session to sand play and another to pitching out of the rough. On the other hand, if you've lost several shots by having to play out of thick rough or bunkers as a result of being erratic off the tee, then clearly you have to practice your driving with woods and irons.

When you have zeroed in on your major weaknesses, you then have to consider exactly which shot you should try to improve. If you're having trouble getting any distance from fairway bunkers, concentrate on doing just that. Take your 3-wood and your bag of balls down to the bunker on the practice ground. Before you start though, be sure to loosen up. You have to stretch your muscles, so that you don't put any sudden strain on them when you swing. Do as you should before teeing off for a round. Place a club behind you and turn back and forward a few times. Swing a couple of clubs to a full finish for half a minute and make certain that you're feeling loose and ready for action.

Now you're ready to begin. But don't just fire off one ball after another off the sand without plenty of time to think about what you're doing. You should pick out a clear target area for each shot and before you swing go through your usual pre-shot routine. Build your stance firmly in the sand and make sure you're properly aligned and set up.

Then after each stroke watch the flight of the ball through the air and decide just why it did or did not bend as you wanted. Give yourself a clear goal. You could decide, say, that your practice session will end when you've hit the target area with nine out of ten sand shots. Whatever it is, make sure you achieve your purpose.

Concentrating on just one problem when you practice often pays off. Just before the 1959 British Open, for example, I was very concerned that I might not even be able to compete. I was hitting every second shot far too heavily in the practice rounds and I couldn't get anywhere from Muirfield's wicked fairway bunkers. So I went down to a nearby beach with my shag balls for a serious practice session. I drew a line in the sand and placed the back of each ball on that line. Then I concentrated on hitting each ball 100 per cent clean. When I succeeded, the line was still there when the ball was flying up the beach. This practice helped me to catch the ball first, not just out of the sand, but on the fairway as well. My confidence soared and I went on to win the tournament.

But as I said, sometimes you have to practice all the difficult shots. Hitting your favorite 3-wood off the tee, or your 5-iron from the fairway may help

you to relax, swing easy and feel good. This sort of practice however, doesn't improve you as a golfer. Face it, you often find your ball in horrible positions: in a clump of gorse, buried under the back lip of a bunker, in knee-high rough, or behind a substantial tree.

These are the shots you must learn to play well - and they can be very stimulating to imagine and execute. So sometimes go down to the practice ground, carrying your bag, and hit balls off downhill lies, or from deep divots, or wander into the fringe of trees and play some from a cluster of leaves, twigs and pine cones.

From a fairway bunker, try hitting some long, high fades, interspersed with low draws, always to a target area and always going through your pre-shot routine carefully before you swing. Visualize the result of each one before you play it, and analyze how effective it has been. The object here is to get a real feeling for every shot, to familiarize yourself with it, so that when you have to play it on the course you will have no problems.

Don't always give yourself a good lie. In a greenside bunker, for example, you should hit shots from uphill lies. Or play balls half-buried under the back lip, or on the upslope when the pin is thirty yards away across the green. And with all these shots you should experiment. Try out the effect of opening the club face a little more, or hitting a fraction farther behind the ball, or taking much less sand.

Your practice session should not be boring if you vary the lies enough. Even though you're practicing for feel, you can still set yourself an attainable goal. For example, if you're concentrating on your standard ten-yard splash shot you can still try and group ten balls, say, in a one-yard cluster behind the hole, never mind sinking one or two of them in the process. You don't even have to aim at the hole itself. You can take any area of the practice green, preferably an area well beyond the hole, which you can mark out with several balls. Then play over the top of the flag, sticking to it until you've landed and stopped six balls within that circle.

This is the sort of game you can enjoy with a partner, for competition certainly livens up any practice, never mind sharpening up your short game. Just spend thirty minutes or so before a round practicing your sand shots with a friend. Have a small bet on the outcome of each shot, or count that the nearest to the pin gets one point, holing out gets five and the loser buys the drinks at the 19th. You will soon find that you're enjoying the time you spend honing your game - and that you're making a lot of sand shots you never thought you could.

The problem with this kind of creative practice is that it can be addictive! It has been for me and it also taught me a real lesson. The more you practice from the sand, the more you wear out your sand wedge. Back in 1961, I had probably the best sand wedge of my life until then and I made the mistake of practicing with it all the time. It finally wore out and there was no way, no welding on of another flange or anything, that could renew it. What I should have done was to buy another one identical to it from the start, using one for practice and the other only for tournament play. If you find a sand wedge that works for you, I recommend that you do the same. You have to really look after your best friend in the sand.

The Practice at Home

So what can you do if you really are restricted for time? How can you improve your golf game, and particularly your sand play, if you've only got a spare hour or so in the odd evening at home? Well, if you've got a patch of sand or a net in your garden, you should be able to slip away from time to time. But if you haven't, there's still a lot you can do to develop your skills, both physically and mentally.

If you want to enjoy your weekend round of golf a little more, you should also consider a bit of exercise. Now I have a life-long commitment to keeping trim. From the start, I had to work at it harder than the average man, for my size (five foot seven) and my weight (145 lbs) were both against me. I ran to build up my legs, up and down the gold mine hills in South Africa. I did thousands of sit ups, squats, wrist curls and endurance exercises. Even now, when I'm traveling on tour, I try to get to the gym as often as I can and work out with the weights for at least an hour.

As you get older, some regular exercise becomes more and more important for your general well being. Even if you're slim, unless you exercise you will not have the agility, strength and coordination that you need for a good golf swing. If you're overweight, you can really suffer from bad back problems, unless you exercise to improve your posture. The reason is that overweight golfers address the ball with their lower spine in an unnatural, concave position, as they thrust their stomachs forward to balance themselves. This stance puts too much weight on the heels or toes, so their legs don't function properly during the swing. Not surprisingly, as a result, performance suffers and so does the lower back.

Clearly, in these circumstances, you should do some regular exercise. You must aim to tone up and strengthen your muscles, especially those that help you to play good golf. Your muscles allow you to start the movement in

your golf swing and you perceive motion through them, which is how you develop feel. This becomes more important with age, as muscle structure starts to degenerate once you are past thirty.

There is no such thing as "muscle memory", a term much quoted in golf instruction, as muscles cannot memorize anything at all. All movement is initiated by the brain and the more a certain movement is performed, the clearer the brain perceives the image, triggering a quicker response. So the more you practice your swing, the more fluid and consistent it will become. Your exercise program should aim to both strengthen your muscles and condition this automatic response.

So what sort of simple workout program can you do to firm yourself up, that is not too tedious or time-consuming? Here's a suggested routine, which will take you about fifteen minutes to complete. If you can do it daily, so much the better for you.

Before you start any exercise session, you must warm up, just as you should before you start to play a round of golf. You have to increase the body's temperature and speed up its heart rate and blood circulation. This prepares you for exercise and prevents strain on muscles, tendons, ligaments, joints, lungs and the heart. You start slowly by stretching all your limbs, making sure you're relaxed, breathing slowly and deeply. You should not lock arms or legs, nor should you overstretch your back or bend over for long periods. You just need to loosen up gently for a few minutes or so.

As a golfer, you have to work on your hands, wrists and forearms to control the club during the swing and prevent the clubhead from wobbling. All you need for your home exercise workout is a heavy book, for a series of book lifts. Just stretch your arms out with the book held between your palms. Roll your wrists up and down some twenty times, holding it firmly. As it gets easier and you progress, you could change to a heavier tome for maximum benefit. You could also vary the exercise by rotating your forearms to the left and then the right, while holding the book outstretched. Do this twenty times to really condition your forearms and build up your biceps.

You can also exercise your pivot, focusing on the correct shoulder turn. Criss-cross your arms across your chest, with your right hand on your left shoulder and your left on the right. Stand with your legs apart, knees flexed, bent forward from the hips as when you address your ball. Then turn your shoulders on a horizontal plane around your spine to your right by 90 degrees, rotating your right hip backwards by about 45 degrees. Hold the position briefly, then swing through so that your shoulders end up at least 90 degrees to the left. Repeat this twenty times. This conditions your muscles and ligaments to perform correctly during the swing and constantly reminds you how it should feel when you swing smoothly.

Swinging a golf club gently and purposefully, where you have the space at home, is also very beneficial. Working on your half swing will condition you to deliver the club face with more accuracy and power at impact. So take your 7-iron and set up to an imaginary ball. Hold the club down the grip a little and bend your knees a bit more than usual. Then swing back with a straight left arm to hip height and swing through to a hip high finish. You should keep your head in line with the imaginary ball and your belt buckle and hands should also line up throughout. If you've swung through correctly, you should be able to see your left palm at the finish. Repeat the exercise fifty times. This helps you to monitor the correct backswing and follow through just before and after impact.

Finally, you must practice the correct turn of your left forearm and the right club path. This is what I call the tee-to-tee exercise. First you have to insert the tip of a golf tee into the top of the grip of a club, say your 7-iron. Then you address an imaginary ball, as you did when practicing the half swing. You swing back, turning the left forearm until the tee in the grip points at the imaginary ball - at this stage, your hands are about hip height. Then you swing the club down and through, turning the left forearm counter-clockwise. You end, with your hands hip high, with the tee pointing once again at the imaginary ball. You should repeat the exercise twenty times, to groove your swing correctly.

Well, that wasn't such a difficult workout, was it? Nor too boring? If you can exercise like this away from the course, your golf would certainly improve. But if you really are too busy to look after yourself, well, you should try to do something to get into condition. Even walking to work, if you don't live too far away, helps. As does walking up stairs in the office, instead of using the elevators. You could also buy yourself a treadmill and set it up next to your bath. While you're running the bath in the morning, you can get on that treadmill for ten minutes. It will certainly do you good.

Exercises in the Mind

You could even spend a little time during the day in "mental practice", which will pay dividends on the golf course. Do you think you know your home course like the back of your hand? Many weekend golfers think they

do, but not one in a hundred has ever worked out a strategy of how to play each hole. When they stand on the tee they are just happy to get a drive away that lands in the fairway, missing bunkers, creek or rough. Then they hit the ball toward the green, hoping that it doesn't fall short into greenside sand, or curl off right into the trees. It's a very hit-or-miss approach that does nothing to improve scoring.

So use your spare time at home positively. Diagram each hole of your home course to start with, marking where the sand and water hazards lie and their distances to tee or green. If the course already has such a printed "par saver" card it's a good start, but that doesn't tell you which clubs you might need to use on each hole in different weather conditions. Think hard about this factor, envision the effects of a strong wind on your drive at certain holes, or how rain or cold could seriously affect the length of your approach shots.

You should also mark in clearly on your plan areas of dangerous rough, which can point out clearly which side of a fairway or green to favor. Note the holes where you do not want to fly over the green and those where it is best not to be short. Difficult greens, with slippery slopes, plateaus or several undulations, should also be charted and, if you can, try and remember the most common pin positions on them.

All this information will stimulate your visual memory of the course and you should then be able to plan to play around it a great deal better. You can decide calmly the holes you can attack and those you should play defensively, which can radically affect your score. For example, before the 1961 Masters I sat down with a pad of paper and a pencil and drew up such a plan for Augusta. I like to attack on all holes, but I know that I must play carefully on those that are very troublesome.

I had started in previous Masters by defending, just playing for pars, but this time I decided to attack on the first hole. It's a 400-yard slight dog-leg to the right, with a large bunker 220 yards out on the right side of the fairway. I made up my mind to hit my drive over this bunker and as close to the green as possible. This strategy gained me birdie threes on three of the four rounds, a tremendous start, which gave me a terrific boost psychologically and quite possibly had an affect on other contenders.

The 11th hole though was one I played defensively. At 445 yards, it has water on the left guarding a part of the green. For my approach, I didn't even look at the flag, as I was afraid I might get greedy and shoot directly for it. I aimed instead for the fairway some forty yards to the right of the green, playing a draw. This brought the ball to a position just off the green, from where I was able to get down in two for par.

This sort of planning is essential if you want to develop as a golfer, and it's fun as well. You can visualize the shots you should make on each hole, and even just thinking about good swings can improve your game. So why not try it? Review your course, work out a clear game plan and then play around it in your mind. This mental "practice" will boost your confidence on the course when you next play "for real" and you will find it easier to concentrate on playing your shots to the best of your ability.

You must concentrate on where you are going to play each shot, not how you are to play it. From a fairway bunker, concentrate on just where you want the ball to finish; from greenside sand, concentrate on landing it softly in your target area and watching it run slowly into the hole. You can do it. You have learned the right techniques of bunker play and practiced them.

You can now concentrate on playing well. The next time you find your ball buried in sand you will have no problem at all.